Lounge to Boardroom

 Inspirational stories of successful South Australian women in business

To be successful you definitely have to stand out, no matter who you are. You have to make a noticeable difference.

BERNADETTE MURPHY (B. 1934)
US chief technical analyst of Kimelman & Baird LLC.
Quoted in *Women of the Street* (Sue Herera; 1997)

ashley knoote-parke

From the publisher

Welcome to our boardroom or, as in some cases, our lounge that now doubles as the boardroom!

Within these pages you will meet an array of fascinating women who have all fulfilled three criteria to be included in this book. First, they have displayed extraordinary determination, second they are making a difference and third they have taken great risks to get where they are.

As one of the most senior contributors to Lounge to Boardroom observed: "You don't get anywhere without taking risks." That particular woman arrived on our shores as a refugee and, as a result, is well versed in doing it tough, but speaking as a fellow "refugee" I noticed South Australian women were way too modest and not prone to making a big deal of what it is they do and what it is they've achieved. This, despite the fact that is IS a BIG DEAL!

I have no problem telling it like it is. I'm from South Africa, you see, where you need a big voice and a loaded gun just to make it through a day and, when I arrived in South Australia, I thought nobody did anything and then I found out that's not true because a lot of people and particularly a lot of women do great things right here in South Australia. But they don't broadcast what they do. So I decided to tell the world, and Lounge to Boardroom was born.

The reluctance of the women in this State to sing their own praises was further underlined by the fact less than 5% of the more than 200 women who were nominated for this book, nominated themselves. And when I interviewed these high achieving women, I was more often than not greeted with the words: "I'm only ..." More like *Only the best.*

I tend to think of this book as a diamond, not only because I regard it as a gem, but because the analogy goes much deeper.

A diamond is many-sided and while every side has its appeal, not every side may appeal to you. So go through this book like a diamond, looking at every facet of what you hold in your hands and I promise you will find the sparkle that resonates with you.

It might be the story of the young woman who overcame debilitating illness to climb dizzying heights of the corporate ladder or it might be the grandmother who is, against all expectations, making inroads with her technological wizardry.

It might be the women who broke through the barriers that others told them were there, or those who launched start-up businesses when all the signs were screaming do nothing.

These are stories that inspire, stories of women who are ignoring the global financial crisis and any other whisper of doom and gloom, stories of women who have changed or are in the process of changing the world.

Join them on their incredible journey and be inspired to achieve because all of the women featured in this book want to celebrate successful women.

One of the first questions you're likely to ask about is the order of the women in these pages. They're not alphabetical, they're not chronological and, in fact, they are in no discernible order, having been selected in a double-blind lottery conducted by the women themselves.

You see, I was so impressed by everyone featured within these pages that I did not want to show any favouritism whatsoever, so around several glasses of wine and platters of finger food we organised an evening of fun to resolve the order to everyone's satisfaction.

It's the way women do things. No fuss, just friendship.

Diamonds, every one of them.

lounge to boardroom team

As with most projects, there is usually a team in the background beavering away to make it all happen. I would like to express my deep appreciation for that team who supported my vision, and who accommodated my strange requests, weird ideas and handled it all with remarkable aplomb. Benjamin, our photographer, who has successfully made us look 10 years younger (thanks Ben); Andrew, our editor, who is the greatest story teller; Kara, the face fairy, who made us look gorgeous, and, of course, our esteemed judges, who had to make some seriously tough decisions as to who made the cut, since the applications were of brilliant callibre.

Thank you all for being part of this inaugural publication and helping it come to life.

Benjamin Liew, Photographer

Benjamin Liew is a young man in pursuit of the perfect picture. His challenge is to tell a story with a single image but to limit the definition of his images to a thousand words is to limit his creativity.

"Words are never enough," is his photo-centric motto, that is continually underlined by the quality of his pictures.

Ben's versatility extends to corporate, commercial, fashion, portrait and landscape photography. His images have been widely published in magazines and books and have won many awards.

Benjamin is a commercial photographer who gets the job done without any fuss.

Kara Fantasia, Make up Artist

As winner of the 2008 Australian Bridal industry Award for excellence in make-up artistry Kara Fantasia is a wanted woman! She is in high demand in both the bridal and fashion scenes working with many top photographers and models.

Kara's expertise in Fashion Styling is also highly regarded.Her 7 years working as a wardrobe stylist at Channel 7 in Melbourne has led to many exciting projects such as working on Melbourne Fashion Week, the TV Week Logies and The People's Choice Awards.

Keep an eye out for Kara's next project "Style Therapy" a styling experience for the everyday woman.

Andrew Tobin, Editor

Andrew Tobin tells stories, some taller than others. Sometimes his own, sometimes the stories other people tell him.

Other than his capacity to write, he has absolutely no redeeming features. Other than the stories he has to tell, he has absolutely nothing to say, although he can say it in an awful lot of words.

When he's not writing he does nothing, particularly housework, which he hates.

Although, to be fair, he does have a fine mind and is great company around a dining table because the only thing he can do apart from write, is talk.

lounge to boardroom judges

With over 200 nominations and nearly 80 interviews conducted, we realised not every one could be in the book. We easily found our initial 50, however, the calibre of applicants was so high, the judges decided to include a few wild cards. And so we selected another 3 women to come in as wildcards and our judges had a even tougher time with the final selection.

The women of South Australia are truly remarkable; they are resilient, modest, tough, determined, willing to dip their proverbial toes in the water, redefine the traditional 'boundaries' and do it all with grace, flair, elegance and refined sophistication. Ladies, it's hats off to you all! Well done and congratulations for making your fellow ladies (and menfolk) all proud!

Emma O'Donaghue - Judge

Emma is an accredited Business Advisor and Corporate Event Coordinator with the Business Enterprise Centre network.

She has been a committee member for Women in Eastside Business for approximately 3 years, assisting with the personal and professional development of business women in the eastern suburbs.

Emma's passion for the support and encouragement of local small business has been the motivation behind the recently formed young business group "Gr8 Business Connections", informing, introducing and inspiring young business people in Adelaide.

Nick Duffield - Judge

Nick Duffield is an engaging public speaker with a wealth of experience in senior executive roles combining superlative negotiation skills and enterprising flair, achieving various career awards including BRW Fast Movers!

Judging various industry awards plus several board positions keep this consummate networker busier than centipedes at toe-counting contests.

Nick enjoys time with wife Amanda and sons Paris & Matisse, savouring snow skiing, gym and the beach; with a notable obsession for Wendouree reds & horizontal ties!

Alexandra Economou - Judge

Alexandra Economou is a journalist at Adelaide's only metropolitan daily newspaper The Advertiser.

After completing a Bachelor of Arts (Journalism) at the University of South Australia, Alex did freelance work for a variety of organisations, including the Law Society of South Australia and Messenger Newspapers. In mid-2002, she fulfilled a long-held ambition by gaining a cadetship at The Advertiser. Since then, she has covered rounds including general news and courts. She currently writes for the business and finance pages, including the popular weekly SA Business Journal section.

Alex lives in Adelaide with her daughter, Olivia.

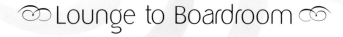

Inquiries should be made to the publisher:

tish'n enigma books,
PO Box 438,
St. Agnes, 5097
South Australia.
e: info@tishnenigma.com
www.tishnenigma.com
Purchases can be made online from:
www.tishnenigma.com or www.loungetoboardroom.com

Photographer, Benjamin Liew, www.benjaminliew.com.au
Editor, Andrew Tobin
Project Manager, Emma O'Donaghue
Malke up stylist, Kara Fantasia
Proof reader, Loana Liew
Cover design, tish'n enigma books
Typeset using Syntax
Printed by TWP, Malaysia

National Library of Australia Cataloguing-in-Publication Entry:

Author:	Knoote-Parke, Ashley.
Title:	Lounge to Boardroom: inspirational stories of successful South Australian women in business.
	Ashley Knoote-Parke; edited by Andrew Tobin and photographs by Benjamin Liew.
Edition:	1st ed.
ISBN:	978-0-9751841-4-1 (hbk.)
Subjects:	Businesswomen -- South Australia.
	Women-owned business enterprises -- South Australia.
Other Authors/ Contributors:	Tobin, Andrew.
	Liew, Benjamin.
Dewey Number:	650.1082099423.

"I look forward to the day when we don't think in terms of a woman executive at all, but just an executive."

Ellen Gordon,
US President of Tootsie Roll Industries.
Fortune (1987)

Kerrie Akkermans & Sue Redman

Sue Redman's attitude to life is: if you're having a good time, it must be good for you. She's been having a great time since she launched *That's Entertainment Coach Tours* at the tender age of 19 and ran it as a highly successful precursor to today's club coach tours, for six years.

From the late night party scene Sue moved seamlessly into public relations fuelled, as she was, by her love for people and memorable events. And she wasn't done as a trend setter either. Sue was one of the first TV celebrity chefs, gaining national exposure on the Bert Newton and Kerri-Anne Kennerley Morning Shows with her decidedly Lucille Ball personality, a heady mixture of zany and corporate canny.

Television, radio and print have all fallen captive to her magnetic personality and for years her book *Creative Cooking with Confidence* has been much in demand.

For a fun-loving, business-minded people-person it was only a matter of time before she launched the hugely successful networking business, *Lunch with Sue Redman*. The only surprise was she waited until 2002 before allowing others to discover just how much fun a lunch with Sue Redman could be! This was followed by 'Beauty and the Beast Business Luncheons' where a prominent male (beast) dazzles his female audience with insights of the business world. The networking opportunity it offers people to legitimately mix business with pleasure has proved an irresistible lure for people to come into the orbit of the woman known as the Networking Queen.

"I believe in a life without boundaries," says Sue, "because it gives me permission to help other people in their journey." And the next stage in her incredible journey is just about to be launched with Kerrie Akkermans. "Together we're double trouble with passion," warns Sue with a smile.

Is Kerrie Akkermans the right person to help you improve your business? Well, if humans are involved in any aspect of your business, then she's the one!

Not surprising to any student of human nature is Kerrie's conviction that the cause and the cure of almost any problem is invariably human. It was through identifying the sameness in people and subsequently the sameness in business that allowed Kerrie to execute her masterstroke – take what she's learned from some of the biggest businesses in the world and apply it to small businesses. After all, reasoned Kerrie, if it works for Amex there is absolutely no reason why it won't work for small business once it has been adapted to match the different size requirements.

So with Toop & Toop as her first client she started Akkermans Consulting in 1994. She has since become a trusted advisor to businesses and a mentor to thousands of owners and executives through training sessions. Kerrie offers clients solutions that go beyond their expectations. The confident Kerrie believes in reversing the risk for businesses using her services – if you don't get results, you don't pay!

For years, Kerrie mixed with corporate Australia, an experience that informed and enriched her activities. Balancing what she learned was a series of personal challenges, including the loss of both her parents and a divorce. Never one to admit defeat, her solution, ever innovative and thoroughly lateral, was to use her experiences to do a stand up comic routine and numerous MC roles.

Her willpower, great sense of humor and perseverance in dealing with the trauma in her life has made her a role model for her two beautiful daughters.

Today her expertise at spotting the silver lining in the darkest cloud and develop creative ideas is much in demand and, along with Sue Redman, Kerrie is preparing a series of workshops encouraging small business operators to get back to basics – performance and profit.

Yvette
Zus Schepel Frahn

Being a farmer as well as a farmer's wife during one of the driest periods in recorded history is not a prospect that would gladden the heart of many girls.

But when Yvette Zus Schepel teamed up with Gary to add Frahn to her already challenging name, it set her on a path of discovery and joy.

"Starting out in our relationship, Gary outlined his dreams and ambitions wanting to know if I would be part of them. I asked him if he was prepared to give up farming to be an artist's husband! He said he was, so we had the basis of a great future," says Yvette only partly in jest.

What has evolved is the dream of one person who, by pulling together a community under duress, is injecting hope where there is often despair. And she's doing it all through art.

Yvette is still very much the farmer who can regale you with fascinating insights into dryland farming, the importance of sustainability and wetlands and eco tourism and her need to leave the land in better heart than she found it, but it's when she is talking about her art projects that she rises to another level.

She's a renowned equine artist who currently has six commissions under construction and while that feeds the beast within that needs to draw and paint she's about so much more than hanging beautiful art on dining room walls.

Yvette lives in the Riverland/Mallee, a beautiful and resilient area that has been particularly hard hit by our dry spell and the cost the area has been paying is so much more than failed crops.

While some are able to shrug and say, well, there's always next year's crop and maintain optimism, others, faced with rising financial pressures, are not merely selling up and moving out, but, tragically, ending their lives and this sense of despair has been filtering down to the children of the area, where the rate of teenage suicide is way higher than it should be in a caring society.

One of the answers, Yvette believes, is art and is doing what she can to promote projects, and teach art in the region that not only literally and metaphorically feeds the very talented band of developing artists inhabiting the region, but also works as a counterpoint to the despair that is stealing lives.

She knows the power of art to revive. "When I wasn't producing art it was like being slowly strangled," she recalls, so to achieve the maximum good for the most people, Yvette has embarked on an almost reverse psychological ploy of focusing on incredibly small projects so that they actually happen and are not forever stuck in the planning, financing and committee stages.

Early in the New Year Yvette plans to change the face of Berri "one paver at a time". Her project, *Growing Rainbows - Little People, Little Pavers*, funded by the Uniting Church and supported by local people and organisations involves replacing the pavements of Berri one brick at a time.

The colourful creations will be made by primary school children before being laid in town streets and beautifully complements the pavement chalk art project in Renmark. "The idea is to get people to stop just an instant longer to admire the colours and change the way they feel," says Yvette.

Her seemingly small ambitions mask a grander design of encouraging art projects across the region such as giant, metal fishes along the Murray and then, who knows that it won't take over the world?

Echoes of from little things big things grow.

Chris Jenner

While most people who experience a sense of abandonment do so as children, Chris Jenner did so as an adult with three young children to care for. While this was more than 28 years ago, Chris remembers it as being a painful and personally devastating time.

The details are another story, but the broad picture is she and her husband, who had been planning a lifetime committed to the ministry, found themselves cut off from everything they knew and living in a caravan wondering what their future held. They determined they had to create new lives, new jobs and new friends.

They've done that and today Chris has a strong presence in the corporate world. Re-entering the workforce as a personal assistant she has advanced her career through study and experience which led to her being "tapped on the shoulder" in October 2006 for the position she now holds as Executive Director of Foundation Daw Park.

Foundation Daw Park is the fund-raising arm of the Repatriation General Hospital and it's been her responsibility to reposition the organisation with the corporate and academic sectors, as well as the military while continuing to nurture and build the community supporter base.

This has required (and will continue to do so) leadership, vision, a committed approach to achieving results, team-building skills and change management mixed with a sense of humour and fun. And it is working! Over the past two years Chris has increased corporate sponsorship support from zero to more than $300,000.

During her 10 years as Director of Business Development in the Adelaide Office of global accounting firm, Deloitte, Chris' focus on account management and the need to build a dynamic broad business network was fundamental to furthering the brand building and profiling of the firm in the Adelaide market.

Through her commitment to community and making a difference, Chris took on the additional role of National Director for Corporate Social Responsibility in her final three years with Deloitte, working with national partners and executives to establish The Deloitte Foundation.

For Chris, this was "an exciting, challenging and fascinating experience" which further strengthened her understanding of and commitment to corporate social responsibility and to community.

It was during these final years at Deloitte that Chris developed a form of cancer that "kept her away from the office" for three months. While this was a stressful and emotional time for her (and her family and friends), she considers herself lucky and privileged to be a survivor; to be able to watch her eight grand children grow and develop, to enjoy her marriage, family and friendships while still contributing to business and community. "I'm very lucky," she says simply.

Her interpersonal skills and judgment have always been rated highly, along with her leadership skills, and her ability to facilitate change and make things happen. She identifies connections and is creative in developing new markets and relationship opportunities.

Her involvement in community, from youth through to her role as Executive Director of Foundation Daw Park underscores her personal commitment to making a difference. A recognised and valued contribution Chris makes within organisations is mentoring and coaching. She enjoys developing talent and believes in helping others achieve their career ambitions.

"Life is for living and I believe in taking it on, beating the odds and enjoying success when it arrives. Along that journey of challenges and success, to be able to contribute to the success of others for me is both rewarding and a privilege." As a woman who brands so effectively, Chris promotes her personal brand through the wearing of memorable jackets. It's a light-hearted signature in a world of seriously serious work.

Paula
Stacey-Thomas

The pivotal moment in Paula Stacey-Thomas' young life was when she watched a chiropractor adjust her mother who had suffered whiplash and chronic pain before undergoing care.

"My eyes popped open when I saw what the chiropractor did," recalls the adult Paula, "and thought it was amazing and from that day I knew I was destined to be a chiropractor."

Her own experience with chiropractic care happened a few years later when she threw back her head at the end of a race and wrenched her neck.

During that healing process the chiropractor also picked up on an accident she suffered as a four year old when she fell off a bike which caused a spinal misalignment. It was a series of events that fixed her destiny in life.

In 1998, as a fully-fledged chiropractor she initiated a project for the Chiropractors Association of Australia, today known as 'Healthy Spines' that she and her sister, Kathleen, have developed into a national program that promotes spinal health to primary school children.

Paula is one of those rare people who was born mature, who always had her eye on the prize and never had to be badgered to study harder, work more diligently, or consider her future.

"I was the youngest of four daughters who were all brilliantly supported by our parents and as a way of rewarding them for the support they gave me, I have been driven to be the best I could," she recalled.

But just because her life lay before her like some yellow brick road, does not mean there were no bumps along the way.

Her confidence took a battering when the clinic she was working in was sold, finding herself without a position a short 18 months after starting.

Faced with bleak prospects in an area she had dreamed of all her life, the young Paula did the only thing any sensible person would in such circumstances – she started her own chiropractic business!

While she might have doubted herself, her parents didn't and it was their encouragement and support that gave her the strength to run two practices – one in Mt Barker and one in Goodwood. She sold Mt Barker and bought and rejuvenated a clinic in Mt Gambier in 2007.

There was a period in 2008 when she would work Monday through to Wednesday in Adelaide then catch an early morning flight to the Mount on Thursday and work there until Saturday then fly home, have Sunday off before repeating the process!

If that regime wasn't staggering enough, the real kick in this story is she did it all with her baby girl in tow!

Today, Paula works exclusively from her Goodwood premises and every Thursday is her designated 'Mummy Day' to enjoy her daughter.

The awards she has won put her firmly at the top of her profession both as a chiropractor and as a businesswoman.

She is convinced her legacy will be the Healthy Spines program that will teach our next generation how and why to look after that most important piece of human superstructure – their backbone.

It's something of which Dr. Paula Stacey-Thomas has in abundance.

Kelly Keates

One day, early in her time at Zonge Engineering, Kelly Keates visited a mining site camp and walked into the mess hall for a meal when one of the men came up to her and said: "You're Kelly, aren't you?"

Kelly was suitably impressed, "How did you know?" she asked. It was one of those lightbulb moments as Kelly looked around and realised she was the only woman in the hall!

Over the years she has got used to her only woman status, as she rose through the ranks of Zonge Engineering to become first general manager and finally the owner. But despite having a woman as owner, the only other female in the company is office manager, Brenda.

"I would love more women to come and work in the mining sector, but for some reason they don't stay," laments Kelly. The scarcity of women in her chosen field makes her even more of an oddity, and not just because she virtually banged down the door of Zonge about 20 years ago to demand a job.

Kelly's appetite for the mining life was whetted when, while at university, she spent her summer holidays working at Western Mining's Roxby Downs dig. She wanted to give it a go and was there for five months as one of two women underground, living in a camp of 500 men and about half a dozen women!

Kelly liked the industry and when she saw the advertisement for a job at Zonge, kept going back until she was employed as an office assistant. The year was 1991 and the office was chaotic. She organised the place, eliminated the debt, made sure bills and wages were paid and her effort was recognised by American owner Ken Zonge who continued to give her responsibility as she set about improving the organisation.

In 2000 Kelly set up the Zonge office in Indonesia. Since then she has worked on recreating the branding and revamping the website. As well, she won for the company a United Nations deal for nuclear testing equipment.

Kelly was made a Director in 1994 and once even quit only to have Ken woo her back with roses!

In 2005 Ken wanted to retire and offered to sell her the company and after some trepidation, she agreed. "It was only after Ken started courting other buyers that I decided I really wanted to own it! At first I wasn't totally convinced I could do it, because I had no specialised knowledge of geophysics but I learned to listen to what Ken didn't say during negotiations! I soon realised I could buy in technical expertise because I was confident in my ability to manage the company."

Kelly's husband and children provide the balance in her life as she rises to the challenge of managing and growing a thriving enterprise.

Under her guidance the company has continued to grow, one day at a time, doubling and doubling again after landing a huge exploration contract that involved Zonge doing surveys throughout Russia, China, Mongolia, and Papua New Guinea.

Today her staff of 35 is more loyal than ever, with crews at mining sites around the country and abroad. She has spent many hours listening, learning and encouraging others to do their best. Kelly attributes a lot of her success to being a tiny, non-intimidating female presence in a male dominated industry.

"No one finds me intimidating," says the 5ft 2" dynamo, who wishes more women would be willing to give mining a career consideration.

She believes she did it not because she's a woman but because she didn't let being a woman get in the way.

Samantha Badcock

Samantha Badcock is a time traveller, one of those incredibly rare people who, while still young, can see clearly the future she wants and knows what she has to do to get there.

She was a teenager who had it all. Nice house in a beautiful suburb, private school, designer clothes, whatever it was her heart desired and a successful dad who took pride in being a great provider.

Then, at 11, she lost it all. Her parents went their separate ways. Next the family business came under intense financial pressure from "the recession we had to have" and at 13 years, while living with her father, they were forced from their home, having to move into a less salubrious suburb. Samantha abandoned her private school for a public education and designer clothes were off the shopping list.

So, did it turn Samantha into a bitter, twisted wreck who lost her ability to believe? Not at all, because she saw the start of her new life as an adventure, an opportunity to meet new people at her new school and cultivate a brand new group of friends. When her parents separated, she remembers very clearly when her mother picked up Samantha and her two younger siblings from a friend's house where the children had spent the day. "All day I had a sense that something was wrong," remembers Samantha, "so when mum picked us up and told us she was leaving dad, it didn't come as a complete surprise.

The younger children, however, started bawling and I tried to placate them by saying it wasn't all bad because now they would get double Christmas presents, one from mum and another from dad. By the end of the ride I had them cheering at the prospect of their parents' separation so I might have overdone it a bit!"

This encapsulates the equanimity with which this mature young woman approaches life.

"The Chinese have the same word for crisis and opportunity, and where some see a crisis, I've tended to see opportunity," she observes matter-of-factly. What that attitude has created is a remarkable young woman who is living proof that youth can be about so much more than smooth skin and shiny hair. As a young and successful business woman inevitably on her way to the top of any ladder she sets her sights on, Samantha has challenged the expectation that age is a condition for corporate success.

"Age has never meant anything to me," says Samantha, "I've always had the attitude that life is about balance. As a result I work hard but equally like to let my hair down with friends and have a natural inclination to give back to society in appreciation of my fortunate life."

At university Samantha completed a bachelor's degree in commerce with electives in Asian studies and, after university, joined the Hong Kong Australia Business Association SA Chapter as a committee member. In search of a career break, she then went door-knocking to find herself a job in marketing. Of course she succeeded because, simply put, the concept of failure does not exist with Samantha.

Her level of community activity also sets her well apart from her peers and includes involvement in a program where she actively mentors a disadvantaged young person and her involvement with the SA Great Speakers in Schools program designed to inspire young people.

Samantha is involved in the *in-business* Young Business Leaders Program through which she is organising a three day trek through the Heysen Trail bringing together senior executives and CEOs. Leading the trek is famous mountaineer and multiple-Everest conqueror, Duncan Chessell infusing a dash of celebrity into the event.

Currently enrolled in a Diploma of Management through AIM and running the SA Executive Division of an accomplished national recruitment firm, her future's so bright she should be wearing shades.

Charyn Youngson

Today Charyn Youngson is Australia's leading home staging professional. She's the expert you call in when you're selling your home and you want it sold for top dollar.

She's not only a published author on the subject and a regular guest on current affair programs, but also a guru to whom people turn when they want help in selling properties for profit.

So how did Charyn get to where she is? Two things happened. One, she got bad advice and didn't know enough to ignore it and two, she got sacked. The bad advice was from a financial adviser who knew nothing about property investment and dissuaded Charyn from buying the four investment properties she wanted and instead persuaded her to settle on one. "I had done my homework," remembers Charyn, "and I knew a property boom was on the way, but the financial planner I'd gone along to see was overly cautious because he hadn't done the research I had, and convinced me four properties would be too risky an investment.

"Looking back, I know I missed out on earning hundreds of thousands of dollars by not following my gut instinct but it really hit home, when I was sacked a few years later, that I had to believe in me.

I saw my sacking as an opportunity to follow my dreams to create wealth through real estate. Instead of going back into paid employment, I invested time and money in educating myself and spurred on with my new found knowledge I risked it all by mortgaging the family home and started to buy, renovate and sell houses."

Charyn's biggest challenge was dealing with the emotional pain of a relationship break up that made her question who she was and where she was going. She admits she lost all confidence and had to reach deep inside to resurface as a stronger, more resilient individual.

"Out of that emotional rebirth came the inspiration to write. I wanted to share my renovating and home staging experiences with a bigger audience. It was a difficult but rewarding journey that connected me with many opportunities."

One of those opportunites was being asked to be a co-author in The Path to Success, a book filled with 55 inspiring stories from highly successful entrepreneurs from all over the globe.

Charyn was then motivated to write her own book, *Sold for Top Dollar - How to Sell your House Faster for More*. This book not only shares Charyn's expert tips and strategies for presenting your house for sale but also guides the reader on how to turn the equity in the family home into a wealth creation strategy that uses buying, renovating, staging and selling property for profit!

In an example of her talent in transforming homes, a recent client of Charyn's made an extra $42,000 when selling his home after implementing Charyn's recommendations over one weekend!

The evolution, from the paint-splattered girl doing renovations till the early hours of every morning to provide for her family, to the savvy businesswoman building a successful Home Staging business is now complete.

In Charyn's fast growing business, Houses to Impress, she is partnered by her daughter Kate and together they have formed a dynamic mother-daughter makeover team. Charyn emphasises her expertise is from hard won practical experience and not some theoretical thesis.

"I am a practical person inspired by ordinary people who do extraordinary things. I hope, in my way, to inspire others to live a life of purpose and passion."

With success comes reward and Charyn chooses travel to recharge her batteries in a variety of locations around Australia and overseas.

Karen Norris

Karen Norris loves the heights. From studying economics after college, her passions were redirected to family, fun, flying and photos.

As a commercially trained pilot and a photographer she has harnessed her multiple skills to forge an enviable lifestyle that has soared to the heights while at the same time brought down to earth the realities of juggling a family, business and artistic talent.

For the past 18 years she has managed a successful aviation training business and since 1991 has built a formidable reputation as a photographer whose work has taken her to four continents and appeared extensively in publications across the world.

Maybe it's the contrast between the sky and the soil but Karen is enamoured of both, flying high in one and capturing the beauty that sprouts from the other.

Many Adelaideans will be familiar with her photography of the book *High Tea in the Garden, inspired by Camellias,* which is now in its second print but many more in Adelaide and around the world will come to know her through the Botanic Photo website.

Karen launched the site in 2005 primarily as an opportunity to share her love of photography with the world, and the world started to take an interest.

In July 2009 the original site made way for its unexpected child – a website where photographers from all over the world can up-load their pictures and those who need to access beautiful images of flowers can go to the site to find them. By far the prettiest portal on the web.

The new site offers very advanced interactive facilities that is really delivering flower power.

From a simple desire to share her love of photography and noting the dearth of pure flower pictures on call at photo sharing sites, Karen came up with the idea of using the internet to market her pictures and those of her selected contributors.

"The internet is such an exciting medium for people who want to start up a business," enthuses Karen, "and it particularly meets the needs of women who, because of circumstances, choose to work from home."

Karen understands well the limitless possibilities of the internet as she employs a personal assistant who lives and works in America and not only performs daily duties for her Aussie boss, but has video skype conferences when needed which enables them to spend valuable "face to face" time despite being separated by half a world.

Into this virtual world, Karen is not only launching many thousands of pictures (she currently boasts an impressive 2000 specialist botanic photos) by selected professional photographers from every corner of the globe (she already has 54 photographers on her books), but also a host of related ideas where pictures of flowers can be ordered to adorn anything from greeting cards to posters and fine art prints.

"While it has taken an investment in time and energy to set up," notes Karen, "now it's in place it is developing a life of its own. The site is constantly growing with the passion of its members and clients. I hope my website will continue to encourage the use of flowers to show some of the beauty of our world."

Karen expects the site will not only be a repository for all things floral, but also a vault to which searchers come and a portal into which they feed requests which are then sent to all the photographers on the data base.

Karen has tapped into an almost primal need for humans to share that of which they are justifiably proud while feeding the other human need for beauty.

Marlene Norton-Baker

Marlene Norton-Baker is a young woman in a hurry. She can already skip across 100m in a respectable 17 seconds but is looking to reduce it to 15 seconds so she can waltz away with the gold medal in her age category at the upcoming World Masters Games.

It will be a natural extension to her stint as a torch bearer during the 2000 Olympic Games when, caught up in the euphoria of the event, she sprinted past the next runner in line at the end of her 400m.

While running fast is no guarantee of business success, it does point to a woman with a sense of balance, mixing the childhood pleasure of competing with a history of successful business development.

In time the rest of the world will come to know some of the truly innovative technology launched by Marlene and her husband under the banner of Proactive Technology Group as companies successfully use the developments to further their own empires.

After almost a lifetime as loyal workers for a number of companies, Marlene and John decided to make serious money for themselves rather than for others and in 2000 bought a desktop publishing business with huge potential that worked primarily with real estate companies.

As new owners they worked hard to overcome many issues and overcome them they did, through persistence and keeping promises they made and grew the business by 200pc. They sold this business in 2003 for a substantial profit proving integrity will outstrip sharp practices every time. "When we bought the business friends asked what we knew about desktop publishing and we said we knew nothing and they were aghast at our decision.

But we didn't need to have the technical knowledge as long as we had the right business practices and staff in place," explained Marlene. And so it proved.

What they discovered in the course of running the business was there were plenty of opportunities ready to be explored and the pair were eager to exploit them. They identified that the internet was the way of the future but there needed to be a better vehicle in which internet users and businesses travelled that highway.

People looking for houses were certainly going to the internet, but real estate agents didn't know how to present the houses. Marlene and John did.

They created an interactive viewing of the house by developing software known as an interactive floor plan and interactive tour. The patent software was designed to meet the needs of the real estate industry and did so with great success.

Taking it a step further they developed Proactive e-book, an Award winning dynamic web based system that delivers real time information, on demand, allowing the viewer to 'page' through publications online. It is proving to be a winner having recently won the AIIA iAwards for South Australia and National Merit iAward in the Tourism and Hospitality category.

Proactive Technology Group became an international company in 2007 when a software license was sold in the United Kingdom. Another product destined to cause a stir is the "myeprofile.biz" which allows people or businesses to present themselves professionally online. In time it will become *the* way in which businesses and professional people advertise themselves.

When Marlene is not growing the next great idea from the Proactive Technology Group and not burning up the track in her quest for gold, she spends her time as a "special justice" that allows her to adjudicate for minor offenses.

And no, the privilege does not extend to passing judgement on fellow contestants at the Masters Games, finding them guilty of minor infractions just so she can nab the gold.

Monica Linford

The irony of a fitness instructor ending up with chronic fatigue syndrome sits heavily on the slender shoulders of Monica Linford. Yet, there she was, exhausted and bewildered and determined to find an answer. "I couldn't help others if I couldn't help myself," reasoned Monica, so in pursuit of the 'physician heal thyself' dictate she set off on a path of self discovery that has enriched her understanding of the human body.

As a classically-trained ballet dancer, a pristine body was always central to Monica's sense of self, so to fall victim to a largely unknown, hard to diagnose and bewildering to treat condition, presented a challenge she absolutely had to meet. The answers revealed themselves as Monica dug into the cause of her condition and today she presents them to people for the truths she knows them to be.

The first truth is "just move" because Monica knows that without movement the body atrophies and the second truth is "everything in moderation". Abide by these two truths, suggests Monica, and you are a long way down the path of wellness. Mind you, the further she delves into these seemingly simplistic statements the more fascinating it gets.

Did you know, for example, that even simple movements set up vibrations essential for the healthy functioning of your internal organs? No? Well, your organs, as well as working together to create a whole, healthy body, have their own lives and their specific tasks and in order to perform them efficiently and stay healthy they need to be looked after individually and each organ needs to be fed its own particular food because each organ has its own capacity to taste.

Appealing to the aficionado in us all, Monica further underlines her lessons by insisting that if we are going to indulge, it should be with quality.

"When you have coffee, make it from freshly ground beans, when it's chocolate go for the best dark variety you can find because when you take pleasure in what you eat, your organs also smile with pleasure. "Equally, when we eat unthinkingly, the organ is flooded and overwhelmed. It then becomes 'injured' and disharmony occurs."

Monica is acutely aware of how different cultures react differently to the body largely because they see it in such different terms. "In the West we see the body as a machine while in the East they view it as a garden," she says and it is achieving a harmonious balance between the two that has driven her to develop a device to revolutionise health care.

It's called a ChiBall and is an innocuous looking, round creation of soft sponge mixed with plastic that exudes a calming aroma and, more importantly, is well on its way to finding itself as a fixture in every home.

The ChiBall is manufactured right here in South Australia and so far has sold 70,000 units in 40 countries. In 2008, with investors on board, a new company, ChiBall World, was registered and now distribution deals have been signed up in the US and Europe.

Enquiries are pouring in from all over the world and Monica and her board of directors are in the process of setting up people in various countries to run the training program, including putting together teams of trainers.

The ChiBall has received official recognition with an award from the Australian British Chamber of Commerce for the most innovative import into the UK and next year The ChiBall Method training program is scheduled to be launched in the US market.

Monica believes, when it comes to wellness, we shouldn't be asking what are you doing, but what are you not doing?

In a few years the only question will be, where's your ChiBall?

Joanna Politis

Joanna Politis is in the beauty business but her passion is promoting the beauty within. Her life is devoted to making the world a more beautiful place by eliminating child poverty and animal cruelty.

Not surprisingly, Jo uses only ethical beauty products on her clients; those that have been developed without causing any distress whatsoever to animals.

"My philosophy is simple. Give the best possible service and make the client look as good as they can, because if you look good you feel good and when you feel good you look good! It's a positive circle."

While today her business, A Touch of Beauty, is one of the best known beauty salons in the State, when she launched it all on her own in 1987 she admits she was too young to know the the fear of failure. Fortunately, failure never came calling and within three months Jo had employed her first therapist and she was away.

Her interest in beauty started with a family friend who was a make-up artist and she undertook a comprehensive beauty course and graduated top of the class. While eager to set up her own business, Jo did the smart thing and went to work in a salon.

She got on famously with the owner and was offered the chance to buy the business. She declined, again directed by her strong business acumen inherited from her parents. Soon she launched her own brand – A Touch of Beauty – a simple and effective name that instantly communicates the nature of the business.

Within a year she moved a few doors down and is still operating today from this salon. Jo has done it all with no business experience, relying on instinct and common sense, and credits her parents with being a stabilising influence.

Jo's campaigning for causes started on a cold night in Aspen, Colorado, the playground of the rich and famous, where she had gone for a skiing holiday, and saw a TV documentary on dying and starving children in Africa.

It started her on a journey she will travel forever and includes support for a wide range of causes and charities.

She is major sponsor of Animals Asia Foundation, RSPCA, AWL, Orangutans in Borneo, World Vision, International Needs, UNICEF, PETA (against the use of animal fur) and also sponsors WSPA, WWF, Wildlife Warrior, JGI and various other charities.

The most significant event in her life has been meeting the extraordinary Dr Jane Goodall DME of the Jane Goodall Institute and Jill Robinson MBE, CEO and founder of Animals Asia Foundation. Both women are passionate about animal welfare, education and the environment devoting their lives to these causes.

"My biggest challenge has been to maintain and grow my business over the past 22 years and to overcome the effects of various economic circumstances. I have kept 10 people employed and have never had to retrench anyone. This success has provided me with the financial ability to contribute to the charities I am most passionate about.

"My legacy is to promote animal welfare and to raise public awareness through better education and communication while, at the same time, giving under privileged children an opportunity to become better educated and valuable citizens in their own communities.

"I adopted a moon bear cub I named Taurus who was rescued from poachers in Vietnam. Knowing he has been saved from the brutality of the bile farms is my reward.

"I am playing my part in saving moon bears from the torture of the bile farms, giving them back their freedom and dignity"

Real Estate Adventures.

How I had fun while making millions in property.

SALLY COUPER

Sally Couper

Sally Couper is a dinner guest to die for. She's bright, generous, interesting and interested. She's hurdled obstacles, risked everything and tells her story in a thoroughly enchanting manner, littered with laughter and bon mots but overriding everything that makes her such an entertaining dinner guest is her capacity to listen.

The ability to tune in to the needs of other people is reflected in her chosen epitaph: *I made a difference – for the better!*

The hurdles she's had to clear have been intensely personal. First there was an alcoholic father who inadvertently fed her negative views of herself then, like night follows day, a marriage to an abusive husband. As a single mother with four children, Sally left New Zealand, the country of her birth, to start life anew in Australia.

Then, one day, she read Robert Kiyosaki's *Rich Dad, Poor Dad* and her life was changed forever. She gave up the insurance industry and moved into property investment. And, as happens so often, when you start doing what you love, life falls into place. A big piece of of her life "falling into place" was meeting the right man, publishing her best-selling book, *Real Estate Adventures*, and building up her and her partner's property portfolio to a staggering 60 properties in three countries!

But the cement holding together all these very significant building blocks is people. The people she knows and loves like her man, her children and her grandchildren, the people with whom she works and the people she meets on a daily basis who come to her looking for inspiration and are keen to tap into her well of considerable know-how.

"I love to see people happy," confesses Sally, "I like to see them move beyond their comfort zone because I know there's a space beyond everyone's comfort zone where real joy is waiting to be discovered."

The space beyond Sally's comfort zone was crammed with the opportunity to infect others with her enthusiasm. To see her being interviewed on national television (which you can by visiting her website) is to witness a woman thoroughly in love with all the possibilities that life has to offer coupled with a convert's zeal to spread the message to those who might otherwise find themselves trapped by a lack of imagination. It's her fearlessness and her humanity that sets Sally Couper apart.

"In life there are no mistakes," she proclaims with a lifetime of lessons behind her, "because you learn from everything you do and an important key to success is self-belief and persistence."

Sally is a huge proponent of financial education, because it enables people to be fully responsible for their own financial well-being, and becoming money smart is one thing she promotes with a great deal of energy and enthusiasm.

In the column of things still to do there is listed plenty of fascinating holiday destinations with her man and so many shops to visit and pretty things to buy in the company of her daughters.

Sally also wants to assist a massive number of people exit the rat-race using property investment as the vehicle

Her website is a treasure trove of information for people keen to make their fortune through property and do it in a way that's ethical and sustainable.

For many people her book has been the jumping-off point for a life better lived and Sally knows it will work as an inspiration for anyone who wants to fulfill their potential.

On her sixtieth birthday in 2009, Sally danced the can can, kicking up her dancer's legs alongside daughters Ayeisha and Truly-Belle and granddaughter Renee.

"See," she says, "you *can* do anything!"

Sue Gibbs

Sue Gibbs' dad was an insurance salesman who had seven sons and three daughters. When he retired, he hoped one of his sons would take over. They didn't so he sold the business. Then, two years later, Sue was recruited by the same firm for which her dad had worked.

"He was flabbergasted," remembers Sue, "he didn't think I had any interest in matters financial because, of course, in those days, women didn't." But Sue did have an interest and an uncanny ability with numbers married to a highly analytical mind which made her perfect for her role as a pioneer in the field of female financial planners.

Undiagnosed dyslexia condemned her to a slow learning path and failing grades so she quit school early and immediately discovered the power of numbers and her affinity with them and the worlds they inhabited. At 18 Sue started with H&R Block and grew the business to six outlets, managing a staff of 40 by the time she was 20.

Marriage, children and divorce intervened before Sue was head-hunted to help set up Capita for Women. The crash of 1987 forced her to change direction and she headed off to university. It was there she discovered her dyslexia but, as if to compensate, found her gift for numbers meant she was the only one in her class who didn't need a calculator and graduated with 100% in statistics!

After university she job hopped, married again then found herself unemployed for four months. A seemingly unsympathetic husband delivered the figurative kick up the backside telling Sue to get off her bum as he "didn't marry her to support her".

It was a make or break moment in their relationship as Sue could have taken umbrage at the unsubtle message and moved on, but instead took it in the spirit it was delivered and set about building her future.

She credits the ultimatum, her husband's belief in her and the never-failing encouragement from him and her children, as turning her life around.

In the real world Sue was drawn inexorably towards the field of finance where she discovered financial management was a natural fit and went on to become specifically qualified.

Having established Professional Choice Financial Services in 2000, initially providing mortgage services and subsequently financial planning services, she could see women hadn't progressed financially in the years she'd been away. Focussing on an education program to empower women to take charge of their finances, Sue set up Financial Choice for Women in 2006.

Her message was as blunt as the advice she was given. "Don't rely on a man for financial security," she says and she should know because "I'm the one picking up the pieces when men stop providing for their women."

Sue's strategies create wealth for her clients. "People often think they need a lot of money before they start financial planning but they don't, they just need to get on with it."

As well as putting into place investment, savings and retirement plans, Sue counsels people to understand the importance of life and trauma insurance.

She further spreads the message by running seminars, workshops and networking functions and gives talks to interested groups – something she would like to do more often because of the need. "My aim is to empower people to be the best they can and break-down the self-doubt that haunts them financially and personally," she says.

Most important of all, Sue has achieved work/life balance by taking every Friday off, with her husband, to be Nanna Sue to her two grandchildren and always manages to fit in an annual holiday abroad.

The feminist surge will crest when a lady named Arabella, flounces and ruffles and all, can rise to the top of a Fortune 500 corporation.

ALMA DENNY (B. 1912)
US writer and educator
New York Times (30TH AUGUST 1985)

Liz Davies

We've all seen those programs on Oprah where someone, usually a woman, has a hoarding problem and it takes 50 trucks to empty the house. Well, the woman who could help Oprah is Liz Davies.

Liz turned her own unwillingness to throw out items that could be reused or recycled into a highly successful business and went on to become the President of the Self Storage Association of Australasia. Developing this embryonic storage business she created, constructed, funded, expanded interstate and now is guiding the next generation of this multimillion dollar business which is underpinning her true passion – changing the world for the better.

With role models such as her father, who obtained a Doctorate in International Law and Economics in war-torn Europe, and an adventurous mother who travelled to every continent from Antarctica to the ancient nomadic tribe of the Himbas in Namibia, Liz learned nothing was impossible.

Leaving the comfort of a highly paid Commonwealth Government job in Canberra she ventured to Queensland and took the first job offered to her in hospitality. Hard work, the ability to listen to what customers wanted and continually suggesting improvements to management of an International Hotel saw her at just 21 years of age joining the board and owning a waterfront home on the Gold Coast.

Realising her career may be limited she returned to Canberra to complete her economics degree, did voluntary work at the community radio station and became involved in student activities.

While trying to understand some of the hardships facing early Australians, she went to Alice Springs and immediately fell in love with the Outback.

She accepted the role of executive officer of the Alice Springs Regional Tourist Association after a stint in Territory Government and her own consulting business. The month her husband and soulmate of 25 years proposed to her, the front cover of *This Month in Alice* showed a large heart – the heart of Australia. She had her children (her "bush babies") in Alice where they grew up and played alongside Aboriginal children and have long-lasting friendships to this day.

Her passion for small business, education and seeking a better future, led Liz to be elected to many boards. In this dusty, male-dominated town, working women did not have many opportunities to meet but, with the help of a group of highly motivated women, a club was formed where her natural desire to teach other people and share her knowledge often led Liz to leadership roles. The Outback taught her with self reliance and engaging like-minded people you can do anything.

With the same fire in her belly and searching for better opportunities for her children the family came to SA in 2000 and started all over again. She immersed herself in voluntary work for local community groups, was again appointed to various boards and her business won Australasian awards.

It is her burning desire to not only make a difference, but to actually achieve her goal of a better world and the absolute conviction that every day is a gift that needs to be shared with others, which turns Liz from an amazing woman into a spectacular example of what can be achieved with a positive attitude.

"I have never measured my success by wealth or power but I judge myself on my continual quest to improve and empower others. Imagine a world where acts of kindness are more powerful than acts of cruelty."

And, as if to underline her belief that we are here to serve and make a difference, Liz has been pre-selected by a major party to stand for Federal Parliament!

Leila Henderson

The first thing you notice about Leila Henderson is the softly beguiling Scottish brogue and the second thing that becomes apparent is it's a cover for her big brain that is in the process of propelling her to the very top of media dealers.

She is one of a few people in an industry dominated by multinational corporations who understands this beast called the internet that giants like Rupert Murdoch are trying to tame.

Consider this for a moment: Traditionally the biggest and most successful companies in the world are those that focus on distribution, obvious distributors such as FedEx, and not so obvious examples of distribution such as Woolworths and Coles, which are actually distributors of groceries. Now, the most efficient method for the distribution of information is the internet, and Leila has devised a methodology for everyday people to distribute information to the media that takes all the labour out of the process.

Her system is called NewsMaker, and is a portal into which people who need to get a message to the world can publish information that is specifically directed to media stakeholders both online and offline – who then broadcast it to the end consumer.

It's like suddenly discovering, as an ardent traveller, you can fly to London for the cost of a bus fare from your suburb into the city.

But she's not sitting back and thinking that's it, I've made it, but is busy tweaking NewsMaker until she's ready to launch the next version, a world first location-based PR service called Globaali ™, which is a Finnish word meaning 'global'.

So watch out world!

How Leila got to the position she's in started with something over which she had absolutely no control – being born a nerd!

She'd read the Bible and the Britannica Encyclopedia before the age of 10 and every day when she hopped off the bus after school instead of going home she went straight to the library – driven there by school bullies.

Her curiosity led her inextricably towards a career in journalism and while honesty is not necessarily a trait everyone associates with people entrusted with bringing us the news, Leila wore it as a badge of honour. "I could be too honest," she remembers, but it didn't stop her rising to the top of the publications for which she worked, in London, Toronto and Sydney.

Meanwhile, she wrote 20-odd books on subjects from sexual health to romance to a history of IBM in Australia and started coaching young entrepreneurs in the ICT industry to communicate their ideas powerfully.

Easily her most glamorous gig was with a travel magazine that took her to 35 countries in two years! However, it was her love of technology that sowed the seeds of what she is reaping today.

She was one of the first journalists to use a home computer at a time when newspapers and magazines were still being put to bed by compositors so when the publications turned digital, Leila led the charge.

From there grew her relationship with all things connected to the internet and the marriage of an insatiably curious mind with this powerful force, well it was always going to produce something extraordinary.

Remember how a short 10 years ago no one outside a fistful of mathematicians knew what a google was but now this word dominates our consciousness?

Well, mark down Globaali as the next word to dominate common usage!

Belinda Wuensch & Cheryl Hughes

The team that puts together the glossy production, *My Wedding Magazine*, shares a special bond – they're actually mother and daughter! When Belinda Wuensch brought along mother Cheryl Hughes to advise her on buying ownership of the magazine, they both thought it was a perfect venture for the other - and decided to do it together. As it turned out, they were right and the two are having a ball growing the magazine from strength to strength.

The pair works well together, with Belinda luring mum from a very successful joint business with dad, where she worked for 25 years, and mum believing she is helping create a future for her daughter in an industry she always believed her little girl would excel. Belinda's degree in visual communications, graphic design and running her own graphic design business for four years was a fantastic preparation for the publishing industry. Also being awarded a South Australian Young Entrepreneur was a handy stepping stone.

Belinda has an understanding of real-life weddings which feature in the magazine - because she has her own classic romantic tale. She met her husband when on an exchange student program in Germany at just 16! "Something as simple as studying German has had a huge impact on my life. Had I not continued, I would likely not have gone to Germany, not have opened my eyes to the world of possibilities and never met my husband. Eight years after meeting and dealing with living on opposite sides of the world, we got married!

"We publish real stories of the real weddings of real people," says Belinda. "My aim with the magazine is to have an impact on people, particularly women, in such a way that they see it is possible to live out their dreams too."

The message of the magazine is simple: *Uniquely South Australian, with creative editorials for brides-to-be on making their wedding day truly special. Real weddings, real honeymoon stories, pre-wedding suggestions and different wedding themes, featuring project ideas for creating beautiful tables, great food and clever bomboniere. My Wedding Magazine is a must-have for creating the perfect SA wedding, from the most elaborate to the budget-conscious.*

And SA brides are agreeing, as they not only buy the magazine (circulation has soared), but a growing number of SA businesses advertise their services and wares within (thanks to advertising, the magazine has doubled in size).

The quality of what SA has to offer to those of us who live here and to the visitors we entertain is a particular passion of Cheryl's. "We want to make everyone realise how special SA is," says Cheryl, with the utter conviction of someone who daily finds yet another reason to sing SA's praises.

"We have a manageable population, good food, great wine, unique venues in beautiful settings, a huge list of top designers, incredibly clever people – we've got it all, just like a country town with the lot!" Cheryl deserves to be honoured as an ambassador for the State she so loves, because not only is she knowledgeable and vociferous about SA, but she is right!

Cheryl continues: "My 'big picture' is to promote our wonderful, diverse State through our magazines – from the iconic Flinders Ranges to the beautiful Fleurieu Peninsula and South Coast, the Limestone Coast in the South East, the 'European-style' Adelaide Hills, Clare Valley and the Barossa Valley, and the contrasting landscapes of the West Coast.

All this, coupled with our architecture and creative, innovative people, makes us a 'special blend' indeed." She laughs at her passion, as does Belinda, because on top of everything, these two are having fun doing what they're doing.

Christine Robinson

Christine Robinson might not be able to turn your pumpkin into a stagecoach or your white mice into fine livered footmen, but as a virtual "fairy godmother" she can transform your on-line business in a way that might well have you believing in magic!

"I've been called a fairy godmother," confesses the decidedly earth-bound and wonderfully centred force whose ambition is to help empower everyone to generate wealth. She emphasises her charter is to generate wealth and by doing so hopes to eliminate "poverty" as a word from our vocabulary and our consciousness.

As with so many women who have found their niche through managing the constrictions life imposes, Christine now rejoices in the freedom she's found after choosing to work from home. From her very comfortable location in the pretty township of Tanunda, nestled in the fertile Barossa Valley, Christine communicates with the world.

"I was just talking to a client in California," she mentions as casually as one might when referring to a neighbour, "developing strategies for her on-line business." And, of course, in today's electronic world, you are the neighbour of anyone with a computer and access to the internet.

The surprising aspect of the business she has built and continuing to grow is that from an SA country town she is the centre of the universe for the hundreds who tune in to her webinars and video tutorials. It's not much different from what she's done in the past, as a teacher, except now she is not limited by the size of the classroom and the number of 'students' who tune into the lessons.

Christine is at the forefront of people who have recognised the world is changing, particularly the business world and while businesses still need to advertise, traditional methods don't work and that is changing fundamentally the way business is conducted.

Into this new world many people stagger, dazzled by the promise of the opportunity but utterly ignorant of how to turn the light on themselves in either their offline or online business.

And into this bewilderment steps Christine, fairy-godmother-like, to guide them, coax and mentor them before finally cheering them on their way.

Christine uses "social media" such as Youtube, Facebook, Twitter and blogs to enable clients to connect to an often unknown world.

"When people first start trying to set up their business on-line, the amount of information available can be overwhelming. If you want to learn a language a dictionary's not enough because it has no context, so I manage the flow of information to enable clients to grow at a pace they can handle.

I monitor their progress and guarantee they'll always have access to someone ahead of the game.- me!" For the technically challenged or time-poor she is also in the business of doing it for them.

People who know something about the internet know they need a presence but a presence without any traffic is about as useful as no presence. "Traffic is the holy grail," explains Christine, "because without it you have no business so I show people how to most economically generate traffic by making them stars in their niche."

But Christine has an agenda beyond simply making money for herself and her clients. "I was in Bali in 2002 during the terrorist attacks and was deeply saddened by the lack of opportunities faced by its inhabitants. I will be going back to teach them how to run internet businesses so they can sell directly to the world and generate a living income."

It's part of her urge to generate wealth so everyone can share in the bounty.

Trudi Pavlovsky

The past is a record of where you've been, not a road map of where you're heading. Trudi Pavlovsky is a vibrant example of not allowing the patterns of the past to haunt your future.

For the record, she states without a hint of emotion that she was sexually abused as a child by three different people on three different occasions. The incidents contributed to her being a withdrawn and aggressive teenager who dropped out of school at the end of Year 11 and then a young woman who entered destructive and threatening relationships.

In her 20s the still unhappy young woman tried three times to end her life, but thanks largely to a mother whose life she strangely mirrored and who taught her daughter everything she needed to know about survival, Trudi emerged from the darkness, determined to be a light for other troubled people.

"I knew my destructive behaviour had to stop as the people who had hurt me didn't care that I was still hurting. I had to find a way to let go of my rage against them and more importantly, against myself, and I did."

Trudi earned her stripes by volunteering for a community mentoring program, while honing her skills and confidence through years of workshops and then working with teenagers in the Teen Life Coaching program.

Now she's launched the Dream Initiative, her own adult-based coaching business that takes people who want to move on from a point of personal conflict to a future without limitation.

Trudi thinks of herself as someone who helps people find their own answers to deep-seated problems. "It's only the way you think about something that happened to you that makes it a problem," she observes in her wonderfully calming voice as she recalls a recent encounter with one of her clients.

"I had been working with this gentleman over a number of weeks and we had just finished our third session when I asked him about an issue he'd raised in our first session, which had caused him a great deal of stress. He paused and said, 'You know, Trudi, I can't even remember what it feels like anymore'.

It was an amazing breakthrough and while the issue that caused him so much pain still exists in his memory, it is not a source of anxiety any more. And that's what we do, initiate processes to make powerful, positive change!"

Trudi emphasises the process is not about masking pain by pretending something never happened, but by experiencing it, grieving and then letting go.

"People hang on to their pain because it gives them what I call a secondary gain, where they use it as an excuse to not deal with life on realistic terms."

Bad things happen but it's important to understand why some people can deal with it and live happy, productive lives while others are caught up in the vortex of destructiveness.

It is Trudi's fervent wish and soaring ambition to help everyone who wants to, to break out of the grip of the vortex.

Trudi believes equipping young people with life skills now will alter their future. "Learning you must love yourself before you can love another is a difficult concept for many."

She attributes her resilience to the example of her amazing mother. "This year, a week before my brother's wedding, her house burned down and she lost everything; yet, at my brother's wedding she was happy, smiling and supportive, seemingly without a care in the world."

Trudi hopes her legacy is being able to help everyone, teens and adults alike to have an amazing life, lived to purpose and with love.

Nicole Sweeny

Nicole Sweeny is a young woman who makes her mark by instilling order and, most importantly, a sense of calm by ensuring business owners understand the importance of a smooth running office; ultimately, changing people's lives.

As a country girl growing up in the Riverland town of Waikerie, Nicole witnessed her family and other small businesses fight through the tough times and steeled herself for success which she tasted early with a scholarship to live and study in Belgium for 12 months.

Moving to a foreign country to live for a year was no small feat for a teenager, while learning another language was a major accomplishment for Nicole.

"My world changed three months into my stay when I started dreaming in Flemish and could hold a conversation," says Nicole cheerfully. After this fantastic, life-changing journey, Nicole moved to the big smoke, Adelaide, where she accepted the challenge of selling door to door – one of the toughest gigs of all.

In time, Revolution Consulting was formed to work with small to medium-sized businesses, specialising in the administration and financial areas. "If those two areas are not working, you might as well shut the doors", says Nicole.

As the managing director of Revolution Consulting, Nicole has helped more than 100 companies operate with an efficiency that is breathtaking. Unsurprising then that Revolution Consulting is positively spinning its way to unimaginable levels of achievement and all on the promise of injecting calm and simplicity into an otherwise hectic work environment.

Nicole performs a forensic analysis of client's data, finding hidden treasures that businesses were unaware of while at the same time noting illogical and inefficient procedures and policies, before developing and implementing systems to solve organisational problems.

"One of my passions is to empower business owners to understand their business and to find their hidden treasures."

Most businesses that fail, do so because the people in control lose focus and subsequently, attention to the essential detail that is necessary for business success. "I remove the pain of paying attention to detail," says Nicole, "while at the same time, promoting focus, which really is a rare condition."

As is the case with many driven, high-achieving individuals, Nicole makes big demands of herself, attempting to take in as much as she can and always focussed on learning from her mistakes.

"Every person I meet has something to teach me," she confesses, "but the hardest lesson I had to teach myself, has been accepting the way things are." "People," says Nicole, "need to learn to not beat themselves up because they don't get everything right the first time. Life is not an explosion, it's a journey and mistakes are all right provided you learn from them."

One of her more memorable successes was when she went into a business, watched and listened to how they did things then simply re-worked their rosters. While that sounds easy, it saved the company a staggering $365,000 a year, a considerable sum when you consider it employed only 20 people!

Nicole has a new project of which she is particularly proud. The company is called Revolution Parfum, and Nicole is confident, in time, it will be a big player in the perfume industry.

But while she's busy building her scent-based empire and expanding her consultancy service, Nicole is conscious of the need to reward herself with the one thing nobody else can give her – time to relax.

"Time is the gift you give yourself," she says, and time is the reward she's earned by starting young and staying focussed.

Angelique Boileau

Angelique Boileau is a pioneer with legend status in the field of female entrepreneurs. She started at a time when most women were forced to be satisfied with office assistant and sometimes rose to the dizzying heights of becoming the boss' secretary – if they dressed right and knew their place.

So when she says "Women can be successful," she knows of what she speaks then adds the insight that comes only with years of observation. "Unfortunately, the men in their lives often hold them back by not encouraging them to take risks and, without risks, you achieve nothing."

Angelique also knows plenty about risks. Twenty years ago, as a brilliantly performing sales person for Konica she was head-hunted by Xerox to take over its poorly performing Adelaide dealership. Xerox not only knew Angelique was a top salesperson, but that her husband was the leading engineer with the same company, and they would be getting a team. After a slight pause to consider what they were risking, the two sold up in Melbourne and moved to Adelaide with their teenage daughters and Angelique's elderly parents to start an exciting new challenge in their lives.

In that time Boileau Business Solutions has grown from an initial annual turnover of $983,000 to close to $15 million in its 20th year, while the workforce has expanded to 42 dedicated team members and, according to Angelique, who is still the company's best salesperson, there's plenty of blue sky yet to fill.

It's been a high-flying journey for this former flight attendant who, as managing director of her own company, has turned pilot to steer a course of up, up and away. And while she's certainly focussed on delivering results to her loyal customer base of about 1600 companies, she's smart enough to realise you can only count on loyalty so long as you are delivering service.

When Boileau Business Solutions started all those years ago all it sold was photocopiers and the only people to whom it was allowed to sell were small to medium businesses. Working within those restrictions has forced the company to develop a sales psychology that focuses on quality because Angelique knows without the attention, the client is likely to wander.

"Our big break came when the photocopier became a multi-functional device of photocopier, printer and fax integrated with the networks of businesses. The year that happened our business, doubled." Due to the evolution of connected technologies, Angelique immediately identified further business opportunities by developing both Telecommunication and IT Services in their suite of offerings to their existing print services clients and thus began a cross-selling culture within the organization.

Today, Boileau is a name most people associate with technological solutions to business problems and, while it really does reek of modern solutions from its impressive new location at the corner of Sir Donald Bradman Drive and Marion Road, there is so much more to Boileau injected by the tireless and almost fervent environmentalist at its helm.

Some of Angelique's passions might at first appear a little odd considering her Hungarian background, her French connection and obvious refinement, but she'll talk footy as ardently as any one-eyed supporter of the Adelaide Crows and the Sturt Football Club; but where her passion merges with her strong sense of community responsibility, Angelique is unstoppable.

Angelique's commitment to animals is commendable. She is an ardent supporter, and Boileau, a long-time corporate partner of the Adelaide Zoo and a leading light in the PandaMania campaign. As chairperson of the PandaMania Fundraising Committee, Angelique helps raise funds for the arrival and residence of the pandas Funi and Wang Wang for the next 10 years.

Anyone who knows Angelique (and that's almost everyone) knows these animals are in good hands.

Deborah Miller

It's rare to find an accountant who specialises in increasing a company's sales figures rather than cutting expenses, which makes Deb Miller a rare catch.

The founder and managing director of Acuere Pty Ltd, Deb, is an atypical accountant whose focus is sales performance "It is," she admits "rare for accountants to focus on sales generation, but my post grad MBA studies took me beyond accounting and into the world of business management."

Deb is keen to encourage change from traditional community models. "We do what we do," she says, "so our daughters and our daughters' daughters can move away from traditional models where opportunities might be denied to them."

It's an indication of the values Deb brings to her career. "Some of us endure the pain for change because a lot of talented women get lost in the current system. Unless we change so they feel comfortable to mix family with career with personal goals, they will continue to get lost."

What are the three top tips for sales growth from this determined woman?

"First is a consistent and repeatable sales process, second is to monitor that process through key performance indicators and manage the results and, third is to get your marketing and sales team to work together." A beaut sound-bite and an indication why Deb is much in demand as a speaker at sales conferences.

The crux of her advice is to increase sales revenue by having a process that focuses on meeting client expectations, while keeping control of the sales cycle. Where there is a strong value proposition it can lead to a higher deal value and result in a higher win rate.

The sensible approach is to select a "niche" market and focus your sales and marketing efforts into these areas to secure a good margin and a reliable customer base with repeat business. "If you compete with the masses your product and services become a commodity and you are left to compete only on price."

The service provided by Acuere is two-fold, the introduction of productivity technology tools, such as customer relationship management systems and emarketing tools and, secondly, through process consulting such as sales training, mentoring and marketing. "In other words," says Deb keen to pare it to its essence, "we offer all the tools needed by a company to create a high performance sales culture."

She is justifiably proud of what her company achieves on a regular basis. "Only the other day I got an email from a client who said their investment with us ($40,000 for a two-week consultancy) was repaid within two weeks as a direct result of the strategies we implemented."

Deb believes relying on change being generated internally is flawed as people are busy and invariably defer or delay, while external consultancy drives change more efficiently through fresh, independent eyes.

Deb has played netball at an elite level where she learned the value of being surrounded by a team, sacrifice for the overall good, hard work and effective communication skills – invaluable skills to take into business.

Another great team she is part of is the one that hops into a car every year in the Variety Bash. Deb has been involved with Variety SA for more than eight years and is a board member. "As you get older you appreciate the fulfilment in giving. When we're in the country and grant some money for an appeal, you see first hand what a difference it makes and it's a fantastic sense of achievement.

So please don't wait till you're older to discover the satisfaction in giving. Remember, life is not a rehearsal."

Taren Hocking

Not every young woman who goes to work for her father covers herself in as much glory as Taren Hocking.

She recognises very well the double-edged sword that goes with the territory of working in a family company, but has used the Dameclian threat as a tool to cut a swathe for herself through corporate Australia.

Admittedly, the Champion Group might well have given her a start and the initial introduction, but the pace at which she has played the game indicates she was a natural.

She started slowly and lowly as a junior, washing dishes and stacking brochures, but soon proved her worth before leaving the family company to prove herself away from parental influence before returning to the fold where she blossomed.

On her return Taren, with a group of notable corporate partners and luminaries including bestselling author and former PM advisor, Anne Summers, created, christened and launched the beautifully titled Serious Women's Business, a forum to "connect, inform and inspire" where notables such as our Governor General, Her Excellency Ms Quentin Bryce, the deputy Prime Minister, Julia Gillard and the international feminist writer, Naomi Wolf are attracted as key note speakers to conferences attended by up to 500 women in senior management positions.

This year she funded a high level symposium on quotas bringing together the nation's leading CEOs and policy makers, and before you think surely that's not needed in this day and age, Taren points out the 2008 EOWA Australian Census of Women in Leaderships figures reported the serious decline in the number of women in executive positions around Australia and she would like to do her bit to raise it to an acceptable level.

The local angle to this success story is that while the conferences are held in Melbourne and Sydney, everything that makes it happen takes place in Taren's Melbourne Street office. She reasons that, with a feminist mother and an entrepreneurial father, an event such as Serious Women's Business was always on the cards! "My father taught me to never give up and my mother to strive to be a positive contributor to our world."

It all started for Taren as a teenager when she worked for her dad in his corporate travel agency while completing her studies. It meant she was exposed to business values and practices at a very young age which allowed her to develop some serious street-smarts. Taren, quite naturally, credits her father Malcolm as her main business teacher and mentor.

Together they launched Champion Events in 1996 and started by following her dad's passion for golf, organising a range of corporate golf-related activities for an array of national clients and brands including the coveted BMW Golf Day. From there they combined their experience in the travel industry to move into incentive programs and conferencing. With the love of all things sport they created Sports Network in partnership with Network Ten more than 10 years ago.

In 2005 they joined forces with former client John Harriss to form the third arm in the group, Champion Sports, a national golf distribution agency, representing international brands including Yes Putters.

The three directors now oversee their own company in the portfolio with Taren's focus very much on the creation and production of pinnacle events.

A particularly big event in the pipeline is the World Wellness Project, a global summit bringing together thought leaders to share, debate, innovate, celebrate and inspire worldwide wellness.

Taren has a simple explanation for her success, "staying focused and positive in the face of challenges. It's not the challenge but our ability to continue that makes the difference. Being surrounded by strong and brilliant women doesn't hurt either," she adds with a smile.

Susan Neuhaus

It's an unpalatable truth that war has given us some significant advances in medicine, when battlefield doctors and surgeons have had to work with incredible constraints under enormous pressure to treat a seemingly never-ending queue of patients in need of emergency care.

Which is why it's commonly acknowledged that a surgeon with battlefield experience is someone who has more than earned their medical stripes.

You won't hear any of these claims coming from Dr Susan Neuhaus, but as one of Australia's battlefield surgeons who has performed tours of duty in hot spots such as Cambodia, Bougainville and Afghanistan, she has seen her share of sights that cannot be recalled in just any mix.

The good doctor is also a Colonel in the Army Reserve where she has been since 1995 and for a total of 25 years she has been serving her country in uniform and with a scalpel.

"The Army has been a keen part of my life, both Regular and Reserve" she recalls, "it has shaped my values and outlooks and opened for me a parallel universe of opportunity." Not just a doctor in uniform, Susan has also taken on significant command and leadership roles for which she was recognised in the Queen's Birthday Honours' List.

Along with these opportunities, however, has been the emotional roller coaster integral to a life of responsibility within the Army.

As with any good soldier, Susan (more officially referred to as Ma'am and not Sir) plays down the more sensational aspects of army life. Her most recent deployment as Clinical Director of the NATO Hospital in Uruzgan Province, Afghanistan saw her in an "operating environment with amazing ballistic protection".

That's code for a hospital under fire, not from bureaucratic razor gangs but rocket launchers and suicide bombers. Certainly, the protection might have been impressive but the fact that people are prepared to die for their cause and even harm those selflessly working to patch up the torn apart surely causes some anxiety, doesn't it?

The Colonel shrugs while the doctor within notes their greatest threat was suicide bombers who launched an attack on a nearby police barracks a few days after she arrived. Not surprisingly, she had an abundance of conflict related traumas to deal with but with one dark overtone.

While plenty of young Afghan boys were brought to the hospital to be treated, she saw only two girls during her time, both daughters of high-ranking Afghans.

But surely there were girls who had been damaged in the conflict? There were. So where were they? While Susan is in no position to confirm it, the only certainty is they were not brought to the hospital for treatment.

When not in uniform, Susan is a clinical academic and Associate Professor pursuing her research into and treatment of soft tissue tumours, rare and complex cancers and melanomas.

It takes her into quality of life issues where, while aiming for a cure, she often has to go beyond a cure point and manage the disease while it runs its course. If that ends with the death of the patient, as it sometimes does, the issue for her as a healer is how to give the patient the best quality of life for the time left to them?

While dealing with that complex issue she is also looking at the critical question, particularly in connection with Army medical staff of 'who looks after the carers'?

"There is an assumption that medical people are trained to deal with bloodshed and untimely death, but ultimately we're human and it does take its toll," says Susan, "and I'm keen to study ways of mitigating that."

Bec Paris-Hewitt

There are some people who have a great idea, mull it over for ever and never do anything about it. And then there is Bec Paris-Hewitt whose capacity to make decisions, and act on it almost instantly is breathtaking in its audacity.

For some, instant decision-making equates with recklessness but with Bec, it is her quick thinking and visionary mind that translates immediacy into almost instant success.

Take the example of her great brand, Zootz. Bec had been in a relationship with her then boyfriend, Kym, a mere four months when they went to have a look at a rarely used nightspot called Zootz at Henley Square.

Over a few drinks with the owners Bec and Kym decided this was it. What could have turned out to be the biggest commercial disaster of her life turned out to be a master stroke as she transformed the gloriously located Zootz from a two-night-a-week nightclub into a seven-day restaurant with incredibly long hours.

She married her boyfriend and acquired a double-barrelled surname but chose to stick with the business moniker of Zootz. Bec and her husband bought the business on December 23, 2003, got the keys the next day, had the place ready by December 24, closed Christmas Day and opened for business on Boxing Day selling snacks.

From that quick start it has grown into one of Adelaide's most popular venues renowned for its functions, cocktails and coffee and closes its doors on weekends at 2am! Zootz is open seven days from 7am for breakfast, lunch and dinner with continuous meals.

Mind you, while Bec made an instant decision to take on Zootz, she was coming from a background steeped in hospitality having very successfully managed quite a few pubs and restaurants.

She learned her trade working long hours making sure other people's businesses operated without a hitch and now she was ready to invest that effort into her own venture.

Not surprisingly, Zootz has gone on to dominate the incredibly popular entertainment precinct that is Henley Square to the point that Bec was recognised by winning the 2005 SA Telstra Young Business Woman of the Year award and the 2004 AGB Suntory Cup State Cocktail champion among other accolades.

It would seem reasonable to assume with the success of Zootz, Bec is a fully occupied restaurateur. Reasonable yes, but not for Bec who is busy growing her empire.

It includes the unlikely venture of face painting and spray-on tattoos under the name of Zootz Funky Faces but it is the story of how Bec got involved that reveals so much about this dynamic woman.

A face-painting friend offered to teach her and mentioned the holy grail of face-painting venues was the Royal Adelaide Show, but getting a stand there was impossible. So straight away Bec organised a stand, then told the friend she needed to learn as she now had a stand at the Show! So every year Bec and her team of face-painters traipse off to the Show for fun and profit.

Amid all this Bec and husband have been busy with their personal lives, including having Jacyb, 2 and Lara, 13 months and enjoying time out and with the help of her mum, to allow Bec the freedom to dream and plan.

When Bec says she's going to do something, anyone who knows her knows it's going to get done. Like the takeaway eatery, Zootz2Go, opening next door, or her promotion of a health drink, Mona Vie the premier Acai organic health juice. She is also a past Vice President of the Asia Pacific Business Council for Women.

For Bec even the sky is no limit.

Jing Lee

Some women are thrilled when people mistake them as being substantially younger. For Jing Lee she needed to be seen as substantially older when she applied for a general manager's position with a multi-national company.

The advertisement, in a Malaysian newspaper, asked for a "slim, tall attractive woman in her 30s with suitable business qualifications" and Jing, just 25 at the time, had no problem fulfilling the criteria of the politically incorrect advertisement with the exception of age!

Young and brave, she showed up to win over her panel of interviewers to become the company's youngest ever general manager. She went on to successfully represent the company's interests in the region.

She's been winning over people ever since and is about to put that ability to the test big time by entering politics on the ticket of a major political party.

She's hoping SA will get behind her and transform this fearless businesswoman into a member of the State Parliament! With her pioneering spirit, there is no doubt she will be breaking down doors and hurdling barriers.

Jing arrived from Malaysia as a non-English speaking migrant but soon added English to the list of languages she had mastered.

As with many, exceptionally bright Asians in Australia, the world of business beckoned Jing Lee and in 2002 she started the consultancy that was to propel her to the forefront of public consciousness.

She found business was a competitive world for which you needed a variety of tools as well as the experience and the talent to pick the correct tool for the job.

The most important tool in Jing's kit is her ears.

It's not that they are particularly big but they perform the vital function of listening and it is only through listening to what people are saying that you can give them what they want. That's true of a business consultant and Jing reasons it will resonate even more for a politician.

"Everything I have learned as a businesswoman will hold me in good stead in politics because I have always believed in speaking from the heart. You have to care about people. Know what's important to them. I believe people will pick up on my sincerity."

On the issue of living with the scrutiny a public persona has to endure, Jing was philosophical, "You have to go beyond that," she muses, "if you let little things stop you, you won't achieve anything."

When it comes to significant achievements to date, Jing helped many Australian companies sign up distributors in the Asia Pacific region worth many millions of export dollars.

In addition to her busy business life, Jing is a strong advocate for multicultural and community development in SA and is a sought-after public speaker and MC for many major cultural and business events.

In anticipation of a political career that is going to change the face of politics, she is not daunted by the expectation. "We constantly evolve as every day brings different challenges," reflects Jing, "getting people on side, whether in business or politics takes a lifetime of cultivation.

My father always said a small tree needs to be looked after every day for it to grow big. Once it becomes big its responsibility is to provide shelter and protection to the many small plants and species growing beneath it.

If you are lucky enough to grow into a "Big Tree" then you must endure strong winds and lightning but also enjoy the glory of the sun during the day and the soft embrace of the moon and stars at night."

Linecke McIlvena

For Linecke McIlvena success in business and involvement in the community are two sides of the same coin, and the more success she enjoys, the more involved she becomes.

Even while running her successful graphic design business, she still found time to help others. She has been involved in many charity and community events, including her present role as chair of North East Women, which helps women in business via networking and sharing opportunities. Linecke always puts others first in whatever she does.

In 2007 she felt she was in an episode of ER. Linecke had gone into hospital for a straightforward procedure, only to wake in absolute agony. An ambulance, sirens screaming, whisked her to emergency where she was rushed into surgery to repair a perforated bowel. As her clothes were cut away in preparation for surgery, she remembers thinking, is this it? For five days she hovered between life and death in ICU, and recovery was a long, slow process.

"It was all very dramatic," laughed Linecke, who has experienced a fair amount of drama in her life, "and as a result my capacity to work and earn was severely limited. It occurred to me that residual income would make a lot more sense."

The need for security resonates for Linecke who, as a child, spent some time in Goodwood Orphanage while her mother recovered from a serious illness. A few years later her dad moved to Darwin to look for work and never returned. While she doesn't dwell on these episodes, there is no doubt they have impacted her life and helped create the caring person she is.

Linecke is compassionate and empathetic beyond measure and reasons that if she needs something, then it's perfectly natural to expect other people to have those same or similar needs.

But while most people stop there, Linecke keeps going, doing everything in her power to help others achieve their dreams.

To that end she has become a star in a technology driven network-marketing company where her focus has been to change peoples' lives, allowing them to dream again. Too often the industry has been promoted as an opportunity to acquire all things material, but for Linecke, it is an opportunity to help others. It is this passion for others that has helped Linecke become very successful.

"My business has allowed me to train and coach people in my organization, and to motivate and train hundreds more through public speaking and workshops.

It is very fulfilling to be able to inspire and assist the people I meet, and teach them how to build a residual income and achieve their goals. Success is the result of changing our thinking. It is a choice, not a chance."

Linecke has expanded her business to provide budding entrepreneurs with resources and mentors, and delivers strategies to enable them to create a life of purpose – with passion.

She hopes people will be inspired to be more, have more, and share their wealth and knowledge with others, modeled on the Pay It Forward philosophy. "I love the diversification that my business provides and I get to meet so many interesting people along my travels. Every day is a fun day."

Her busy life has included raising two beautiful children, and is focused on empowering people to change their lives for generations to come.

In two short years, Linecke has built her cash flow positive business to a point where she is a consistent leader in the Asia Pacific region, and continues to expand rapidly and impact lives around Australia and internationally.

Blis Bohunnis

Blis is an artist. She is inspired by the magical potential of water to recreate balance and buoyancy within the inner life of her clients; body, soul, heart and mind. Blis is a weaver of dreams.

A master of real magic giving a gift that lasts. Her early exposure to quantum physics, Buddhism and psychotherapy and her early career as corporate coach have honed her skills to bring together the esoteric and business worlds.

As a corporate trainer of trainers Blis has empathy for the challenges that face high flyers. For 21 years Blis has been the warm wind beneath the wings of more than a thousand world-weary clients and has inspired them to heights of personal genius and integrity of identity both personal and professional that they had not dreamt possible.

Her art is the power of calm and her method is to tap into the seam of life's golden silence to recreate the flow of serenity.

Acqua Blis is a private Spa Sanctuary where one can experience the blissful lightness of one's own being. Blis discovered the magical potential of water to recreate balance.

Water facilitates a re-birthing into an inner world where the secrets of healing are found. Her constant presence as coach and confidant enables a remarkable sense of both comfort and intimacy. It is the vibration of nature that heals.

The pinnacle experience is the client being floated and cradled, spun around and even sung to in the ozone spa with birdsong, breezes and dappled sunlight playing on the water.

The effect is one of both intoxicating relaxation and euphoric motivation.

From the moment one enters the enchanting Eastern suburb's English country garden, in Adelaide, South Australia, one experiences the hush of a sacred sanctuary. Her warm embrace welcomes one home and the journey begins as one remembers who one truly is and where the infinite possibilities of life's potential resides.

Blis has dedicated her home to her consultancy with a massage room, spa and sauna retreat and the reflective Buddha garden with the avenue of white flowers and rolling lawns.

Blis' client base is international. Her clairvoyant "over the phone" coaching has liberated the genius potential in lives of actors, singers, producers, authors, poets and entrepreneurs in London, New York and Paris. Blis speaks fluent French and with this skill she translates her client's hidden potential and life purpose in more than one language.

Blis' journey into an authentic way of living and being began with the fear of expressing her clairvoyant power, shutting it down and thereby denying her gift to the world. Her immune system created energetic blockages manifesting as tumours in her jaw bone.

She elected to be conscious during each and every one of the 22 operations. She chose to understand the tumours not as the end but as the beginning - the beginning of putting all her faith in the magic within.

Blis' clairvoyant insight is both refreshing and astonishing in its ability to fast track results. This unique healing modality is a fusion of creative ability and the science of the Vega machine.

The primary purpose is to raise the vibration of each clients' energy so that they may realize their full potential in all aspects of life.

"I want everyone to go beyond their own fear to shine," says Blis. "By my shining and fully showing up in life I give permission for everyone I connect with to shine."

> " *There is no glass ceiling. My gender is interesting, but it is not the story here.* "

Carla Fiorina (b.1954)
US chairman and CEO of Hewlett Packard
'The Century's Business, Career and Money Sheroes', Society and Politics (2000)

Jan Wood

Overcoming setbacks to identify and service a vital niche market in an aging Australia are the hallmarks of a hugely successful business that could operate as a blueprint for any burgeoning entrepreneurs.

But while Jan Wood and her husband, John Minchenberg, are enjoying success now, it wasn't an easy ride to the position of unlimited potential they now enjoy.

Jan's company is called Healthcare Specialty Products and while today it has all the trappings of success, she and her husband have endured a relatively rough ride in finally establishing the business.

It is the third incarnation of a venture they launched many years ago sourcing mostly furniture items for healthcare facilities. Jan's background as a nurse positioned her well to identify the very real needs of the needy and, talented with keen business acumen, she spotted a market for quality furniture that met specific needs.

But even such a simple idea met resistance. When Jan approached manufacturers to make lounge, dining and occasional chairs to particular specifications designed to make life more comfortable for the elderly and the slightly infirm, most resisted, preferring to stay with the range they knew and confident people would make do with what was offered. However, the three or four manufacturers who were open to her suggestion are today elated with the increased business they have won by following that ridiculous principle of giving the customer what they want!

Jan then went the next step and followed one "crazy" idea with another even more preposterous one – service. "Too often healthcare facilities found once they'd bought a particular item they were abandoned by the person who sold it to them, but we believed in service and, as a result, we have been rewarded with repeat orders," recalls Jan with some pride.

A practice that underlies Jan's mantra of looking after her customers brilliantly is her refusal to pursue an order when the person for whom the chair has been ordered dies. "People need to grieve and they need space in which to grieve and they don't need to be hounded into paying bills at such times," says Jan. While the business "wears" any financial setback from these unfulfilled transactions, the reward is the goodwill it generates from its consideration. Not so satisfying have been the business arrangements, made in good faith, but not adhered to by other parties that caused pain and distress to Jan and her husband.

Her response has been to focus on her own development by undertaking an interior design course, to be completed this year, so she can offer qualified advice to Healthcare clients. It's a way of value adding to the great service already on offer.

Today Jan and her husband have almost more business than they can handle but understand the importance of doing it right and recognise they are the best people to guarantee the continued success of Healthcare Specialty Products. "We are good at what we do," says Jan with modest understatement, "because our passion for what we do comes from deep within."

That passion is driving the company into expansion mode and it has recently appointed a Victorian agent who will be modelling their successful strategies in SA and NT with a view to repeating that success in Victoria and after that, who knows? Jan almost certainly does but she'll talk about it after it has been done rather than telegraph her moves.

One move she will talk about happily is her planned holiday to Vietnam in the New Year which will be the couple's first in five years! Judging by the speed at which their business is growing it might also be the last holiday the pair take for many years to come.

When Jan is not growing her business, she attends dressmaking classes, cooks up a storm, relaxes at the theatre and fusses over her two cats and two dogs and seven grandchildren.

Corina Kowald

There are many ingredients that contribute to a brilliant life. There's stoicism, tenacity, persistence and courage, which can all help you leap any obstacles that fall in your path.

For Corina Kowald it's all that but mostly her lust for life and an almost reckless self-belief that is rewarding her with abundance in all the important facets of a life well lived.

On the surface she appears as a woman who has come through with grit and determination, surviving a vigorous business baptism. Consider the annus horribilis she endured in 2008. At the start of the year she bought a house only to watch interest rates rise a staggering five times in a row.

The economy took a severe downturn and people simply stopped buying and her landlord told her the shop rent was going to double – end of discussion!

She and her photographer hubby, whose work had also dried up, were desperate, drowning in debt and close to throwing it all in.

So what they did was put into action a saying of Corina's father "when the going gets tough, the tough get creative" and they invested almost the last of their savings in a two-day course to learn meditation!

And, as strange as that might sound for some people, it worked a treat. They meditated an hour a day for six months and in that time and since then, their lives have turned around.

Corina quit the over-priced shop and moved into another down the road which has served her purpose so much better. Now Corina is smart enough to know meditation didn't alter the world, but rather altered the way they viewed the world and with their new world view she and her husband turned into a couple of winners.

It gave her focus and firmed up her view of her ideal customer with enormous clarity. "She's a woman in her 30s to 60s who loves to pamper herself and her loved ones and who appreciates excellent quality service," recites Corina.

An army of such women have been flocking to her exquisitely presented shop in Willunga called *I am Tall Poppy* where they will find irresistible unique luxury giftware, homewares, fashion, accessories, babyware and children's toys.

While this only child of German immigrants has come a long way, she knows there are many roads waiting to be travelled, some in the strictly corporate world where she would like to see a chain of *I am Tall Poppy* shops espousing her philosophy as well as breaking into niche markets with one-off products that create a buying frenzy, preferably via her on-line presence and all this balanced with time for her children, her garden and her pets.

"My reward is my relationships, be they with my husband, my family and friends, my customers and business partners and my animals. The spiritual component of all these relationships is vital to my well being and I feel books like this one are really important because I have always been inspired by other people's success stories. I take the attitude that if they can do it, so can I, and if I can help some other person battle through tough times and never give up, then I am so grateful for that opportunity.

"Because I've always wanted to be a good example for my children, keen to help them grow into strong, independent people who take responsibility for their actions and respect themselves and others, what I would love to impart to all is you should live life to the fullest.

"The keys are love, happiness and abundance and everyone needs to know there is plenty out there for all, including you, because you deserve it."

W = V × L

DEALMAKER   TRADER   ...TOR

YOUR LIFE
YOUR LEGACY

Judy Hamilton

For Judy Hamilton it might have seemed early on that life was always going to be as pretty as a picture. After university she maintained her links with academia by working in an academic library as a qualified librarian.

In 1978 she was appointed the first woman registrar of a State Art Gallery anywhere in Australia. As the first female at that level she enjoyed the position of privilege revelling in the picturesque beauty her job afforded her. She stayed for an impressive 23 years and during that time assumed the role of Acting Director of the Art Gallery. Also in this period she journeyed the seemingly predictable path of love, marriage and motherhood and then the not so fun but rewarding role of single mum.

When Judy chose to end her time at the Art Gallery it was because she had developed an interest in personal development, and had completed a post graduate diploma in clinical hypnosis and became a reiki master specialising in stress management. And Judy knew all about stress, having had to manage 40,000 works or art and a multi-million-dollar portfolio!

The stress of all that responsibility plus the ongoing demands of single parenting was damaging her and she had needed to learn how to manage it. What she was particularly attracted to were the natural techniques for managing stress and, once she had mastered those techniques, went on to teach them to others.

It was during this period that Judy realised that, in spite of this, she was approaching burnout and left before the demands of the job could destroy her.

Once she had acquired, part time, all the necessary qualifications to enable her to promote and teach stress management and having had herself as the perfect, totally stressed out subject, she took a separation package from the Art Gallery and concentrated on her healing practice.

She taught reiki and healed herself by healing others who came to her.

Over 10 years she built up a formidable reputation and a loyal clientèle before returning to the world of corporate employment, but still with the healing arts.

She took on the role of regional manager with a specialist medical college and in the three years she was there became a certified coach and trainer in neuro-linguistic programming or NLP, a system of alternative therapy which seeks to educate people in self-awareness and effective communication, and to change their patterns of mental and emotional behaviour.

Then came the big light bulb moment in her life when she discovered Wealth Dynamics – the profiling system for entrepreneurs, and the global social entrepreneurship organization XL (which stands for eXtraordinary Lives).

Ever the pioneer, Judy wanted to bring XL into Adelaide, as it was the only capital city in Australia where it wasn't operating. In 2007 she bought the XL city licence for Adelaide and in early 2008 Adelaide won the award for the best growth in the world for a new city.

Judy impacts a lot of lives and helps a lot of people who are ready for transformational change. Knowing her Wealth Dynamics profile changed everything in her world and gave her the understanding of her place in this life.

In future Judy plans to take Wealth Dynamics into businesses so they can build the right teams to grow effectively, and help people get to where they want to be. As the recently appointed Business Development Manger at Sirdar Adelaide, she was on track to do just that.

A particular passion is to work with women stuck in jobs they hate, to create a double benefit of helping the individual as well as the company be happier.

Wherever she goes, Judy is inclined to take the positive picture with her.

Lynda Croser

When you think of farmers' wives running businesses, you're unlikely to think first of fashion. Yet fashion it is. The inspiration, energy and drive behind the iconic SA owned, clothing label Live Life Designs, is the enthusiastic Lynda Croser.

While working as a young sales assistant in a fashion house Lynda awoke early to the revelation that success comes to those who meet the needs of others.

The label started as a small, home-based business in 1990 when Lynda, as owner and designer, combined her love of people and fashion to launch a stylish range that catered for the busy and diverse lifestyle of Australian women.

"It has never just been about clothing," confesses Lynda, "but also about helping people feel good about themselves and allowing their inner beauty to shine through."

The label is available in three exclusive Live Life Designs concept stores around the state and to the world via a glossy mail-order catalogue and the internet. The stores are located in areas that offer a unique shopping experience; the picturesque tourist town of Penola, the seaside holiday destination of Robe and on the Norwood Parade in Adelaide.

Live Life Designs is a vertically integrated business as the collection is developed from the ground up from fabric selection and designing, through to production, and on to marketing and retail. "It's an exciting industry," admits Lynda, "which is constantly evolving and we're fortunate to have such a great team.

I consciously chose likeminded people to populate our stores because I wanted them to mirror my own attitude towards giving customers a remarkable shopping experience." And it's worked, with customers commenting on the in-store experience – different in each location.

Lynda is particularly proud when customers make a point of visiting each of the stores where the ethos is the same but the visual stimulation and ambiance reflects the store's location. "Each store has its own personality and customers enjoy being a part of the story and the growth of the business," she says.

Live Life Designs promotes two ranges, Live Life Woman, which focuses on key wardrobe items and Live Life Spirit which caters for the young at heart with a more daring, fitted and fresh fashion edge.

Live Life Designs has customers who are drawn to the label because of the unique styling - expressive colour, attention to detail and the ability to create a personal look.

While the business has developed steadily to its present status Lynda has always kept things in perspective and family is her priority.

Her appreciation of life took a giant leap forward when her then 16-year-old son broke his neck in a motorbike accident. Thankfully, he made a full recovery which, to Lynda, felt like a miracle and taught her to not worry about the small things.

"I have always been a grateful person," reflects Lynda, "because I felt gratitude enriches you and engenders a sense of positivity that enables you to create your own reality. Life really is a journey and when we travel a little bit every day, it's amazing to reflect how far we've travelled."

Her entrepreneurial flair and courage in pursuing her dreams has rewarded her with the "luxury of self education and the opportunity to meet wonderful people" to the point that today she can't recognise herself as the person who started Live Life Designs.

Drawing on her personal and business experiences, Lynda has learned to motivate and encourage others to have a go. The key to success, she believes, is being passionate about what you do and combining the qualities of determination and fearlessness.

Michelle Stanton

Michelle Stanton is a woman who has already achieved everything but is only just beginning to flex her considerable influence. These seemingly contradictory positions make complete sense once you grasp Michelle's breathtakingly simply philosophy – it is as it is.

It took a serious, life-threatening illness for Michelle to realise that she did not need to struggle in order to be successful. The year was 1995 and Michelle's family and medical carers were deathly afraid Michelle was not long for this world.

But it was while in this parlous state that Michelle experienced a state of being, which she describes as a state of wholeness where nothing is missing – there is no senses of wanting or needing anything; there is no sense of insecurity or anxiety.

It is a state of deep inner peace, love and joy. A timeless state of being, which she later called Being in the Zone – the same state that champion athletes are in when they perform extraordinary feats with absolute ease.

For a period of eight years, Michelle was unable to work due to ill health. During this period, she spontaneously experienced many months of living IN the Zone alternating with months of living OUT of the Zone (the normal, stressed state she used to live in prior to her hospital trip). Unfortunately, having experienced the joy of living in the Zone, being OUT of the Zone became unbearable for her. She knew that she just had to find a reliable way to step into the Zone and to live consistently in it.

After about a decade of research, Michelle discovered a fool-proof method of stepping into the Zone. She called it 'Sensing What Is'. "Whatever it is that is happening in this moment, be aware of it with all your senses," says Michelle, "this brings you instantly into the Zone".

About a year later, Michelle discovered the triggers that throw people OUT of the Zone and how to dissolve these triggers.

Michelle called the method of identifying and dissolving these triggers "Debunking". "There's little point in achieving a state of joy if you very soon fall out of it and don't know how to find your way back," she says with all the practicality of a woman who has spent more than 20 years as a high achiever in conventional business.

Michelle has tertiary qualifications in science, education and marketing and worked in senior management positions at ANZ and ICI before taking on the challenge of small business!

Having tested the efficacy of these two tools on a couple of hundred people, Michelle wrote *The Timeless World – Debunk Your Fears and Discover Heaven on Earth*. She then commercialised her business in Adelaide in mid 2006.

Since launching Zonehigh, Michelle and her growing team of Zone coaches have helped hundreds of people in business and every walk of life, achieve extraordinary success without feeling any pressure or stress.

It is Michelle's vision to grow the Zone community globally to help create a world that is peaceful and harmonious where people don't suffer a sense of separation and lack. "The first thing you want to do when you feel bad is to hurt people," says Michelle, "and we're about making people feel good so they do good spontaneously."

Michelle emphasises that the process is simple and the rewards instantaneous. "There is a false belief that happiness is a by-product of achievement, but what you discover is that you can have happiness now no matter what your circumstances. And when you are happy, material success is a natural by-product."

The growth Zonehigh is enjoying is testimony to its appeal and its effectiveness.

Suzette Khodair

There are many who want to be stars and many more who are happy with anonymity but every now and then you run into someone strangely anonymous who has star quality exuding from every pore. Say hello to Suzette Khodair, an extraordinary individual, all embracing and utterly uncompromising with a heart that would surely dwarf Phar Lap's.

This woman, who could be running countries, has instead over 30 years created the best deli, then the best Continental deli, followed by the best gourmet deli, then the best gourmet deli and coffee house and today the best gourmet caffe in the world!

It's a bold claim, but it doesn't come from Suzette, rather from the people who frequent Suzette's Gourmet Caffe and if it was possible to measure such achievements it would register off the scale.

But while Suzette today exudes all the trappings of incredible success, the truly extraordinary aspect of her achievements is the journey she has endured.

Blessed with a mother one could only dream of and a father sketched by Dante, Suzette was born into a culture where women were valued on a par with donkeys. With seven children in tow, Suzette's mum travelled to Australia to meet up with her husband who had emigrated five years earlier. It was not a happy reunion and the burden of looking after the family fell to Suzette. "You are the man of the house," said mother to Suzette reflecting the values of her homeland Lebanon and heaping praise and expectation on the 15-year-old shoulders of Suzette.

But take on the role of principal bread winner she did, leaving school and starting a regime that would buckle most beasts – 15 hour days, seven days a week!

It wasn't so much the hours because, as Suzette reveals, she has energy to burn, but as well as running the family deli, she and her mother had also bought a fish and chips shop across the road for dad who developed the habit of telephoning the deli to ask for Suzette every time a customer surfaced and Suzette was effectively running two shops while literally running between them. The stress of supporting such a large family and being the principal carer for a younger brother were impacting on Suzette.

But worse was witnessing her parents' disintegrating relationship and being subjected to her father's attitude that he didn't need to work so long as he had daughters who could be his slaves. It finally pushed Suzette into a nervous breakdown at 18 and a six month stay in Brazil where, for the first time, she got to be a young girl doing all the things a young girl should.

Her spirit restored she returned home to resume caring for her family and running the family business. By now, dad had been given his marching orders so, without that burden, Suzette was able to devote all her considerable energy to simply running the business which grew and evolved with the tastes of society.

Supermarkets sprouted to squeeze out old-fashioned delis so she turned Continental then the Garibaldi small goods affair poisoned that market so she was reborn as a gourmet deli before, in time, adding a caffe to it and finally, abandoning the deli to unveil Suzette's Gourmet Caffe. Along the way she had her battles with landlords and Councils but really, they never stood a chance.

She still puts in 15-hour days, seven days a week and the reason she will succeed in everything she does is because of this: "My purpose is to help everybody," she says, "I have a lot of love to give."

It's a short step from Suzette's Gourmet Caffe to whatever world Suzette wants to conquer.

Irena Zhang

South Australia's Central Market and Chinatown precinct is one of the most diverse, vibrant and harmonious communities in Australia and Irena Zhang's influence can be felt throughout - from the white guardian lions and gates we walk by, to the fusion of Asian cuisines we eat and the dynamic success of those community organizations that have flourished under her leadership.

Irena is widely known as a generous, compassionate, inspirational and a highly regarded business and community leader. She has a long record of outstanding business success and has displayed limitless enthusiasm to nurture and contribute to SA's highly envied multi-cultural and dynamic business environment. She is a driven entrepreneur who is culturally aware and sensitive to the needs, expectations and business practices of various European and Asian groups. Irena's diverse business portfolio includes her role as the Managing Director of Dasina Pty Ltd. a management company that operates the International Food Plaza in the heart of Chinatown.

Irena came to Adelaide as a non-English-speaking migrant and is seen as a role model by the encouragement, mentoring and support she has provided to newly arrived migrants, international students and those most vulnerable in our multicultural society. Irena is an in-demand keynote speaker and regularly addresses multicultural and ethnic interest groups.

Irena has a passion for the arts and has curated a variety of multicultural and community focused art exhibitions, internationally acclaimed dance and theatre performances and is known as a catalyst for fundraising activities and events for wider causes outside her local community that have included the Adelaide Zoos "Pandas on Parade" project, the 2009 Oz Asia Festivals "Journey to the West" performance, Sichuan Earthquake Appeal, the Guangdong Flood Victims Appeal, The Premiers Olympic Games Appeal and the South East Asian Tsunami Appeal.

Being born into a family that celebrated the arts and literature, Irena developed a love for the fine arts, antiques and French Provincial Furniture. To come away with a deeper impression of Irena and her love of the arts, things of wonder and objects of desire, one only needs to visit her unique and welcoming furniture business: Novaline Furniture.

Irena's willingness to contribute to the general welfare of our society can be illustrated by her long-term commitment to the following community focused organizations: past board member of the Council for International Trade & Commerce SA, Vice President of the SA Council for the Promotion of the Peaceful Reunification of China, Board member of the Overseas Exchange Association of Guangdong Province, Past President of Chinatown Adelaide of South Australia Inc. and the current President of the Australian Asian Chamber of Commerce and Industry.

In July 2009, Irena was elected to the 340 Executive of the All-China Federation of Returned Overseas Chinese; she was 1 of the 15 delegates from Australia whom joined more than 1,100 representatives, including celebrities, senior CCP party officials, and newly returned overseas Chinese, who gathered in the Great Hall of the People, Tiananmen Square, Beijing to attend the Eighth National Congress of Returned Overseas Chinese. Irena was the only woman representative from Australia. Nine members of the Standing Committee of the Communist Party of China Central Committee Political Bureau were present at the meeting. During September 2009 Irena was awarded the Council for International Trade and Commerce (SA) Awards Outstanding Long-Term Contribution award and the Chinese Migrant Elite Business Award at the 3CW Radio 10th Anniversary Celebration & Chinese New Migrant Elite Awards.

This exemplary record of achievement in the community is a testament to her ability to foster and maintain harmonious, genuine inter-personal relationships and her ability to build "cultural bridges" within our multicultural society.

Sally Curtis

Sally Curtis, the entrepreneurial connector, has the gift of perception, to see people and businesses as they *can* be, and brings together the right people, at the right time for the right opportunity and she does it all with light- hearted, genuine selflessness.

This extraordinary woman uses her talents under her brand, Twisted Connector, to link you with whoever is most likely to make a deal successful for both parties.

So what is an entrepreneurial connector? Sally explains: "I help people find and develop their right teams. You are only ever one connection away from the person you really need, a person who usually makes a significant difference to you and your business. I make those connections for you through referrals, identification, education or connecting."

In a life that is increasingly being filled with successes, Sally regards her most significant as "finding, accepting and celebrating me". This insight has propelled her to bigger and better connections, allowing her to value the one link common to all her connecting – Sally Curtis, the Twisted Connector.

Before evolving into a presenter of brilliant business solutions, Sally was quite the conventional daughter, wife and mother. That was until the rock in her life and her inspiration, her mum, suffered a stroke and Sally was forced to find herself.

Then, 13 months later, her marriage ended. "It was a time of massive pain," she remembers, "but then from massive pain you experience massive growth."

Sally has an incredible team of key connections and resources around her and she is willing to share and assist those people who will genuinely benefit from them.

The team has a global perspective of business systemisation and strategic development and provides cutting edge, innovative steps to move from one arena into the next with ease and efficiency.

An example would be taking a business with an unclear vision, provide it with clarity through questioning and strategic processes then building a bridge with steps on how to take a business to the next level, and more importantly doing it!

To understand how Sally's talent is putting together people for their mutual benefit, let's hear from someone who has used her service: "Sally thinks very quickly in each moment, scanning her memory for other people she has met that might either need what I have to offer, or who might have what I need in order to solve my problem. In a flash, the suggestion is made and the potential connection is crystallised.

Sally brings people together in a way that flows with the universe. She is part of the flow, no constraints, no selfish agenda, just a massive desire to help others. Sally is a witty, light-hearted, loveable, sensitive person who makes a major difference for people who are open to 'The Twisted Connector touch'."

The testimonial is one of many that sing her praises.

Her legacy will be providing people with the knowledge and skills to step up in life and trust in themselves even when they go against the grain, knowing that the dots will connect perfectly in the end.

"The trick is to make every day a play day," says the energised Sally, "and you do that by loving what you do and doing what you love.

Celebration is an integral part of the process and it's important to celebrate the little things and, most importantly, having a team with which to celebrate ."

Xenia Ioannou-Mena

As the child of parents who fled to Australia as refugees, Xenia Ioannou, is convinced she must have picked up on their sense of total loss.

She arrived in Australia as a four year old with parents whose combined wealth was $200 and whose total possessions were enclosed in a suitcase but whose responsibilities extended to the two children they had brought with them.

As well as starting over in a new land, what mum and dad did was inculcate in their children that the way to secure their future was through property ownership. It was a lesson the young Xenia learned well for, despite acquiring multiple university degrees, Xenia started on the path of property investing when she was just 19. "My parents instilled in me that wealth comes from property. My father used to say university will give you an education but real estate gives you wealth."

Xenia used DNA technology to create vaccines and despite 9 publications in medical journals, believes the psychosomatic component of illness is too often overlooked at our peril.

While she worked at her scientific research, Xenia kept building her property portfolio but could not find someone to manage her properties the way she believed they should be managed and, being a logical person, reasoned that if she was dissatisfied with what was on offer then there must be other property investors similarly disaffected.

So she left the lab behind and, while raising her three wonderful children, launched AdProp.com.au, a property management company that understands investors and today has a substantial rent roll managing properties from Gawler to Aldinga. Xenia is also a director of Adelaide Property Finders, a buyer's agency run by her husband Angelo Mena that sources, negotiates and purchases investment properties on behalf of investors.

"Wealth creation is a mindset," argues Xenia, who strongly believes that "wealth is a value that you create in yourself." The incredibly positive Xenia believes growth brings happiness and all we need to do is decide the area we want to gain success in. She's chosen to grow by helping other people achieve their full potential. "I want to be known as a millionaire maker," she says, "and the way to do that is to rewire people for success. "Every person is a potential genius and can gain unlimited potential by tapping into the personal power they have always had."

Xenia places a lot of emphasis on the power of the mind and, in addition to writing a book on the subject, runs the *millionaire mindset master class*, a workshop focused on the science behind success.

She believes that most investing strategies and courses can work, but investors need to develop themselves before they look at developing properties. "It is happiness that brings wealth."

Xenia firmly believes that personal growth depends on who is around you. "Life is a game," she reflects, "the bigger you play the game the more you understand it, the more you get back in return." Surrounding yourself with the big players provides room for upward growth."

That's why Xenia runs the Real Estate Wealth Network, a business that gives South Australian investors an exclusive chance to learn from the wealthiest people in the world.

"The seminars provide powerful wealth-creation strategies and are advertised through our AdProp newsletters." Investors also gain essential network opportunities. "I feel it is important to allow everyone a chance to speak because great ideas are often developed as a result of bouncing them off other wealth-minded people," Xenia says.

It's a philosophy of abundance that is propelling Xenia to the forefront of wealth-creation strategists.

Karen Martin

Karen Martin always knew the answer lay in science, but just wasn't sure about the question.For five long years she stared into a microscope looking for evidence of how the behaviour of a single cell might be responsible for triggering chronic disease, but changed direction when the idea of blaming a single cell didn't hold all the answers.

Without being fully aware of what she was doing, she was letting her instinct guide her towards a more holistic approach. Still holding onto her scientific roots she virtually stumbled into an area that 20 years ago was little acknowledged by the scientific community. "At that time, naturopathy was considered very "alternative" and was associated more with commune lifestyles than with legitimate healthcare practices," she recalls.

With hindsight, naturopathy seemed the most logical step for this achiever. Undaunted by the common perception of naturopathy, Karen envisioned a "merging" of the two, where scientific enquiry could be used to validate natural health practices. The use of scientific evidence to support clinical practice is an area which Karen has worked strongly to promote within the naturopathic profession. "In clinical practice, we need to know whether something works or not, how it works, and whether it has any potential to harm.

This way we can make the most appropriate treatment choices for a client." Twenty years ago there was little scientific evidence for complementary medicine practices, but today there is a wealth of information which is growing every year. This validation has also increased the status of complementary medicine in the eyes of medical doctors, some of whom now even refer clients to a naturopath.

Karen saw in naturopathy the potential to make an enormous difference to people's health, but she was concerned with the lack of recognition it received. In response to this she embarked on a career path which saw her combine many professional roles. She established herself in clinical practice, involved herself heavily in leadership of professional associations, advocating increased professionalisation of complementary medicine practices, lectured naturopathic students, introducing scientific enquiry to the curriculum, administered naturopathic colleges and was appointed first lecturer in Naturopathy at UniSA in 2003. "When I started on this journey the education of complementary practitioners was not cohesive, there were different curricula and varying education levels. Today we have University degrees in areas such as naturopathy and acupuncture."

Karen also contributes to public education and awareness through public lectures, radio and media articles. "I believe the public need to be able to make informed choices about complementary medicine, and should expect professional treatment and service."

Karen has served on many advisory boards and in 2008 was appointed to the Complementary Medicines Advisory Committee which advises the Therapeutic Goods Administration on Complementary medicines in Australia.

Most recently Karen has focussed on clinical practice, establishing the Australian Centre for Natural Health and Wellness which is a multidisciplinary complementary and allied health clinic. This clinic is unique in that it combines complementary medicine practices such as naturopathy, acupuncture and massage with allied health disciplines like psychology and dietetics in a functioning professional team, rather than simply cohabitating practitioners.

Although treating all health problems in both males and females, the Australian Centre for Natural Health and Wellness is regarded as Adelaide's premier clinic for Women's health, fertility and natural IVF support. Fertility is an area where people are increasingly turning to natural therapies, and Karen and the other clinical staff have a proven track record in this area.

"My clinic is the culmination of what I wanted to achieve. It is professional, well run and highly respected. It demonstrates that it is possible to integrate complementary and allied health as a team in order to achieve the best outcome for the client."

Ann Grenci

Sometimes where we are needs to be measured against where we came from to fully comprehend the enormity of the journey. Ann Grenci is a woman who seemingly has it all and has done it all.

As a young girl she grew up in a household where her mother and sisters endured domestic violence and were not valued because they were females.

Her constant deeds have been directed at bringing inspiration and value to the life of others not so fortunate and who have walked through similar circumstances.

The life she has today is happy, fulfilled and balanced due to the influence of her grandparents, extraordinary mother, amazing sisters, family, incredible friends, colleagues and mentors who have been integral to the happiness she now enjoys.

Ann's experiences have engendered in her a finely tuned sense of empathy that is constantly opening doors to give entree to troubled lives. "I have trained refugees from Africa who witnessed parents and family slaughtered in front of their eyes. They have opened their hearts and homes to me and have felt comfortable to confide their horror stories. I like to think it is because I am able to build a rapport and genuine friendship with them by treading softly and building confidence and self-worth gently."

Ann is an educator with TAFE and the WEA and knows life is so much more than can be found in books and that most learning takes place while you are busy living.

She is a highly disciplined, multi-skilled educator and training specialist with an outstanding history of trail-blazing – always finding herself at the cutting edge of innovative approaches to vocational training.

Her extensive experiences in small business and industry set her apart from her peers as does her natural ability to network with all sectors of business, industry and government departments. She has spent 30 years inspiring, motivating, role modeling and demonstrating that with persistence and dedication anyone, irrespective of their origins can overcome obstacles and achieve.

"My insatiable drive and positive mindset stems from my strong belief that everyone needs a dream and enough belief in their unique abilities to fulfill that dream, be it big or small."

Ann's current work focus is in the area of *Recognition of Prior Learning*. She boasts many examples of exemplary practices, forging partnerships between industry and the education sector. In 2008 she credentialed staff through the *Recognition of Prior Learning* process through TAFESA which resulted in a Café achieving finalist status in the Restaurant and Catering SA Awards for Excellence in the *Professional Development* category.

While Ann's life has been a steady climb upwards she regards the day she started university as perhaps the most significant turning point in her life. Her journey has not been easy. She has had steep mountains to climb and poisoned rivers to cross but believes "lived experience" is the greatest teacher and that one can also learn from the experiences and trials of others.

Having empowered herself with empathy, compassion, skills, education and lifelong learning practices, her mission is to continue helping people explore their potential and hold on to the belief that anything is possible. "Ignite that desire to make it happen," urges Ann, "regardless of obstacles and maintain a sense of humour. I like to continually challenge myself to think outside the square."

Ever the diplomat, she points out that the only person standing in the way of whatever it is you want to achieve is you, so change and help yourself.

Nicole Fleet

In one form or another Nicole Fleet has been jumping out of airplanes for as long as she can remember. Sometimes metaphorically and often literally.

Sky diving is her out-of-work-hours passion and she has the distinction of being part of a four generation jump when she leaped out of a perfectly good aeroplane with her father and grandfather.

And the fourth generation? Young Harry, who'd been growing inside her for 11 weeks at the time of that jump and "enjoyed" a total of 22 jumps before mum reached the cut off point for pregnant jumpers! He's now one in real time and mum has taken another leap of faith by moving her very stylish florist business, The Blu Tulip, to an exclusive on-line presence.

The last jump was, in fact, about reducing risk rather than keeping fingers crossed the parachute opens, and had made The Blu Tulip not only more competitive but freed up Nicole to pursue the corporate market for her blooming business.

"We recently secured the Rydges as a corporate client," said Nicole referring to the prominently positioned and newly renovated resort at the corner of South and West Terraces.

As well as adding large, corporate clients to her portfolio, Nicole is keen to create a marketing initiative that turns the buying of flowers into a natural activity. Thanks to her vision, the fourth week in every month has been designated "Blu Tulip Week of Thanks" to allow everyone to show their appreciation via specially priced blooms.

"I want to encourage people to say thank you to someone in their lives who least expects it," explains Nicole. The feel-good factor of the exercise is that a donation from every order will be given to Variety SA.

Nicole's work ethic and zest for business was sown in her from birth as she helped her parents on their potato farm.

It was an idyllic life where Nicole wanted for nothing and the sense of satisfaction she derived from participating in the family venture set her up for a lifetime of not shirking hard work.

Her innovative approach to business was developed when, as she studied at university, she taught herself massage and set up her own massage business.

When she completed university Nicole continued her massage business and started working for Executive Fitness Management launching one of its corporate sites which she built up over a period of eight months.

She was thrown in at the deep end and added to her client list by cold-calling employees to promote the advantage of fitness. She was still running her massage business at the same time and it became so successful, Nicole damaged her wrists and had to sell the going concern!

While sky diving has been a shared passion for her and her partner, it has also helped inform her business practice.

The habit of getting jumpers to pack their own parachutes was adapted to a mantra of personal responsibility in all her business dealings where she has shone by putting into place systems that deliver.

"When the new site is launched it will offer customers the chance to not only pick the flowers they want but also to select a card and even write their own message, all online! It's a sales system of which I'm particularly proud."

Wherever she's worked Nicole has increased the efficiency of the business by introducing systems and is confident the ones she's put in place to run her online florist from the new warehouse premises she's wisely sharing with the delivery company, will carry it to dizzying heights.

Mariana Pavic Disanto

When Mariana Pavic Disanto bought her first house the new dining table almost touched all walls in the dining room. "Why did she get such a big table?" asked one of the delivery men of Mariana's mother who was home to receive the table. "Oh my daughter," answered mum, "she says her first home will not be her last." Mum's daughter was a girl with big dreams. At the time she was recently married with no children and only had a casual job.

Today, 18 properties later, she has seven children, runs four businesses and the once huge dining table looks like a coffee table in their current home and is not large enough to accommodate the whole family!

Home is Barton Vale House in Enfield that is not only the Disanto family home, but also one of the four businesses Mariana runs as Barton Vale Events.

Mariana's background is of the utterly normal variety and, in fact, borders on Dickensian. Her beloved dad died when she was just 11 and her mum raised her while surviving on a pension.

There was not much money for luxuries and early on Mariana determined she was not going to be restricted by a lack of money so started working from the age of 13.

She worked every weekend and school holiday through those years, mostly in sales, starting with selling lollies door to door and then selling leather clothing at the markets.

She talked to the "luckier" kids in school and asked them what their parents did and while still a teenager joined the dots to work out that property equaled wealth.

When she was 16 she suffered another close loss, five years and five days after her dad died, and that taught her about the uncertainty of life and the need to do your living now and not put it off to a time that might never come.

Today her life is occupied, with her seven children, the many properties she owns not only in Adelaide but in Queensland and New Zealand as well and the mortgage broking business, Financial Prospects, she runs to help other people with their property investing, while her creative side inspires her and her equally creative children to plan their own businesses and make jewellery to sell at every opportunity!

When she was 12 she discovered a pendant in her jewellery box on which was inscribed the words *Live. Love. Laugh*. This had a profound effect on the young Mariana who 23 years later still cherishes the treasure. Her life has taught her to add a few more mantras, some of her favourites being *Follow your dream wherever it leads: don't be distracted by less worthy needs: shelter it nourish it help it to grow: follow your dream wherever it goes; Don't cry: Change it; The world is at your fingertips and Success has its own rewards*.

She's lived by these words and uses them on her children and husband when tough love is needed and Mariana knows her success has delivered her the most cherished of rewards in her children. "It was almost as if fate was saying you've worked hard so here's your reward, each time I was blessed with another child," laughs Mariana.

But has she finished working to achieve all her goals and has she had all her children? "I want to continue building my property portfolio around the globe and build my School of Dreams that inspires all children with their families to succeed, however they define success and when I look around my beautiful family and I have a sense that not everyone is here so until I feel that everyone who should be here is here, I'd like to leave it to fate and am open to welcome more children!"

And one is left with the very distinct feeling that whatever Mariana sets out to achieve, this utterly remarkable woman will achieve. You pigeonhole her at your peril because she shatters stereotypes and makes you realise anything is possible.

"The test for whether
or not you can hold
a job should not be the
arrangement of your
chromosomes."

BELLA ABZURG (1920-1998)
US POLITICIAN, LAWYER AND CAMPAIGNER.
BELLA! (1972)

Colette Smith

There's an element of *so what?* when reflecting on Colette Smith's achievements. Sure, she's young for the lofty perch she occupies with one of Australia's largest employers – Telstra – and while that's deserving of applause it sets no records.

No, you have to dig a little deeper to discover the treasure here because at first glance she's merely a woman who's done well but when you look at the journey it assumes epic proportions.

At 17 this Year 12 student and former gymnast was told she had an acute case of arthritis affecting all joints and would be confined to a wheelchair from 25 onwards. She never went back to that particular specialist, refusing to accept a diagnosis that was at total odds with the way she saw herself.

But as unwelcome as the diagnosis was, she credits it as the turning point in her life. "It brought me to my knees," she recalls, "because I'd planned to study dramatic art and become a stage actor."

But she didn't stay long on her knees, recalling the words of Jim Rohn: *The heavy chains of worry are often forged in idle hours*, she got busy working out what she wanted to do and how she could go about acquiring the skills to do it.

What Colette did was the stuff of novels. She went to America where she acquired incredible life skills by constantly challenging herself. She focused on the task at hand and her attitude changed.

She grew in confidence, learned to be streetwise and adaptable, and, most importantly for her later life, how to win at sales. She opened herself to the mindset of success.

"I placed attention on what I *could* do," she says, "I set goals and took small steps to achieve them.

My development was incremental and the more positive I felt, the greater my sense of achievement became which enabled me to take on bigger challenges."

After absorbing everything positive she could from her American experience, Colette returned to Australia and worked as a carer for three years looking after people with head injuries. She then went through another major flare up, was assessed unfit to work and put on a permanent disability pension. Four weeks into that phase of her life she got a job in a 300-person Telstra call centre.

From that point on Colette never looked back, realising the many opportunities available in a company the size of Telstra, especially for someone who had a clear vision of what she wanted to achieve and the ability to do so.

In the next 11 years Colette had seven promotions and relocated with the company to Melbourne, regional Victoria and finally back to Adelaide.

Today she finds herself as General Manager, Telstra Consumer Adelaide. It's been a fast climb and Colette is appreciative of the opportunity offered her by Telstra in return for tenacity, dedication and consistently high sales performance. "I never made an issue of my health problem, in fact, rarely mentioned it and because I didn't, neither did anyone else".

Not surprisingly her inspiration is people who have overcome adversity and her artistic parents, "beautiful, humble people who don't get caught up in the material rat race".

In both her personal and work life, Colette likes to be seen as someone who leads by example, achieves what she sets out to do whilst staying true to her core values. "If there's any difference I would like to make it would be to help others see their own potential.

I believe it's possible to always improve a situation by taking accountability and giving something a go."

Kathy Fullston

Sometimes things you don't want to happen and don't expect to happen do but it's how you deal with misfortune that distinguishes you from the ordinary.

The extraordinary Kathy Fullston is a pioneer reshaping the world while dealing with the global issues of climate change and toxic chemical overload. Into this titanic struggle exploded a personal tragedy when her heavily pregnant sister and brother-in-law ploughed head first into another vehicle and were killed.

"You can dwell on it and it will drive you insane," says Kathy, "or you can accept it happened, acknowledge you have lost people you love deeply, and move forward."

Her moving forward is an ongoing battle with the drought and a countryside into which untold gallons of chemicals have been poured. Kathy is the co-manager of the family farm, a third generation holding defying trends in particularly dry times. SA is enduring arid days and the Mallee is renowned as a singularly waterless region, so how is this young woman turning Cloverland Organics into a cashflow positive enterprise? With courage, conviction and exceptional managerial skills.

The courage and conviction kicked in because they were bucking trends that said the answer to diminishing crops was even more chemicals and the exceptional managerial skills identified future markets that would sustain them when traditional income streams evaporated.

"We started addressing our carbon footprint when the phrase meant nothing to most people," explains Kathy, "best practice farming coupled with native trees was an obvious solution." Ironically, their motivation was not pecuniary but altruistic as they were setting out to save the world by making their little piece of it respectful of its environment.

What started as a favour to the world is turning out to be a life saver for this pioneering farm.

Their vision is to have 75pc of their holding growing native, bio-diverse plantations creating future habitats. Carbon sales from these plantations will be used to further improve degraded areas.

The 5700 acre farm Kathy and her husband took over, along with the surrounding farms, had been degraded by poor farming methodologies and the family's health had been compromised by excessive exposure to chemicals. "It was an easy decision to go organic" says Kathy, "when you realise it is the last resort to a healthy lifestyle. Farmers' wives are leading the charge towards healthier farming to counter current practices that impact adversely on health and environment."

Kathy is adamant. "The farmer's primary source of knowledge has been tainted by agricultural scientists becoming involved in commissioned sales of agricultural chemicals!"

For Kathy, going organic has resulted in healthier crops and livestock. The explanation is as simple as it is obvious. "Livestock will eat whatever grows on our land, even so-called weeds, because natural fertilising enhances palatability. On neighboring properties the imbalance creates toxicity in weeds and livestock avoid them. That means even through the drought our herds have increased."

As well as carbon credits, Kathy's farm is developing its trade in organic meat, delivered to the door of people keen to ingest organic cuts.

Kathy's vision comes from a deep sense of responsibility to humanity and she does what she can to improve our environment. In time, she plans to turn her farm, a mere 26 km out of Murray Bridge, into a health retreat and is already laying the groundwork by encouraging health-conscious campers to holiday amid the native vegetation.

Then there are the plans for the Organic Grill high in the treetops where people can feast on clean food and plenty of oxygen … and the ideas for enriching the world keep flowing from this amazing woman.

Donny Walford

If there were speed limits on the rate at which you live your life, Donny Walford would be weighed to a standstill by the number of tickets plastered on her.

This dynamo lives her life at a million miles per hour as she challenges perceptions of what it is women should do and are capable of doing.

By her own admission, Donny operates at break neck speed because she "doesn't know any other way" and she can trace the start of the race to her dad, her hero, who held down three jobs at any one time, while she inherited her genetic blue print from her mum who, after a full day volunteering at the local church or school would still be awake past midnight making sure the house was spotless.

Donny grew up thinking it was natural for girls to do whatever it was that boys were busy doing and when she went to join her brother and his mates in a game of cricket on the playing fields at high school, the reaction from the girls taught her all she needed to know about peer pressure and the place of women.

Since then she has been leading a joyous charge to redefine the place of women in society and particularly in business.

As with most people who have lived or are living full and fulfilling lives, Donny has endured and triumphed. Her darkest moments were intensely personal like when her dad died while trying to set up a faulty electric barbecue and a short time later when her only brother was killed in a car accident.

Her biggest triumph to date has been the four years she spent assisting the Bank's executives in turning around the fortunes of the then State Bank of South Australia after it crashed so spectacularly in 1991.

It was a furnace that steeled her and forged her into the formidable force she has become but it is her attempt at reshaping women in business that Donny hopes will be her lasting legacy.

Behind Closed Doors is a support network for business women that currently operates only in South Australia but soon, thanks to Donny's vision, will be a national network designed to promote the notion that women can achieve anything and need to help and encourage each other to do it.

Through the Behind Closed Doors program Donny will encourage members to support Plan Australia with its new campaign – **Because I'm a Girl**. Members will be part of this world wide campaign to make a difference and raise awareness for greater investment in girls to help end the generational poverty cycle that exists in developing countries.

Making Behind Closed Doors possible is the company Donny started in 2006 – DW Bottom Line – that helps companies and individuals focus on the things that need to be done to improve their performance and hence bottom line and be hugely successful in business.

Having proven herself a genuine achiever in all things business, Donny is now busy not only expanding her empire but proving to herself she knows how to enjoy the harvest she is reaping. To that end she is in a relationship with her dream man who is teaching her to relax and, like everything else in her life, she is taking to it with aplomb! Family and friends, keeping fit, champagne and aged reds are on her "most enjoyable" list as is the little sports car she zips around in – but not at breakneck speed!

On her headstone in a time far away are the words: "Donny lived".

In August 2007 Donny won the Asia Pacific Business Council for Women "Woman of Distinction Award" in the Economic Development & Investment category.

Tansy Boggon

Tansy Boggon recognises that each of us needs to follow several paths to achieve optimum wellbeing. As the wife of a prominent chiropractor, Tansy could have considered chiropractic as the only path.

Being a health conscious and pragmatic woman, however, she set about creating Health Zone, a business offering natural health solutions to people with a variety of health goals.

With a background in conservation management, Tansy has been busy building the business model since the beginning of 2009, harnessing the talents of six wellness practitioners under the Health Zone brand.

Tansy expanded and relocated her husband's successful chiropractic office and saw an opportunity to further assist clients on their wellness journey.

Due to her dedicated efforts, Health Zone now offers Pilates, nutritional consultations, remedial massage, yoga and counselling services.

Her vision has also seen corrective chiropractic and Pilates unite to create a new approach to optimal spinal health.

Health Zone now combines proper alignment of the spine to ensure maximum nerve flow, with a balanced muscular system to provide long term health benefits.

Health Zone is unique in offering this combined approach to wellbeing. Tansy, a trained Pilates instructor as well as the centre's business manager, has been developing short Pilates sessions specifically to complement corrective chiropractic in addition to the regular Pilates classes.

The priority at Health Zone is to encourage people to initiate preventative healthcare measures.

Since Tansy recognises that preventative health can be challenging to market, she has endeavoured to ensure that Health Zone is at the forefront of the community's awareness.

Health Zone promotes healthy living by sponsoring community events, venturing into gymnasiums where they offer free posture checks, scheduling open days and providing the centre for complementary workshops.

The innovation Tansy brings to her current business pursuits and the culture of inclusiveness can be traced back to her alternative parents who raised her on a sustainable farm.

Her enterprising father built their home from stone sourced on their property and recycled material.

Her childhood was spent appreciating nature's innate intelligence. Ever since, she has worked with nature to facilitate its natural inclination towards harmony and balance, rather than struggle against the natural order. This holds true with the philosophy underpinning Health Zone.

Tansy is justifiably proud of the harmony collaboratively orchestrated at Health Zone. "We often receive comments on Health Zone's positive and calming atmosphere".

This has facilitated exceptional health outcomes for clients of Health Zone.

"It feels that I am at the right place at this stage in my life," she says "I enjoy applying my skills to help create a healthier community."

Andrea Petersen

Sometimes you just have to shake your head at the way things work. As a young chartered accountant, Andrea Petersen went to work for Relationships Australia, a not-for-profit organisation that offered marriage guidance where she spent three years being indoctrinated in the way of all things not for profit.

At the end of that time she realised there was a real opportunity to make a difference in a sector with a staggering 700,000 not-for-profit organisations, many in dire need of sound financial management.

And that's only in Australia!

But there were a few personal hurdles to overcome such as postnatal depression that stalked her for five years after the birth of her son. She resisted the drugs because she felt they were not for her and looked to start up her own business as a form of therapy to try to conquer the depression.

"Starting up a business requires your complete concentration and I thought it would be a great distraction from the ineffable sadness that was swamping me," she recalled. While her marriage didn't survive Andrea had obviously picked up something valuable from Relationships Australia and today has a mutually supportive partnership with her son's father who, she says, is a terrific dad and friend.

The year was 1999 when she started Not for Profit Accounting Specialists and the business has grown 25 per cent a year for every year of operation. A success no matter how you count it. Apart from using it as a tool to battle depression, Andrea started her own business because she wanted to build an income stream that wasn't dependent on her presence.

But financial security is only a small part of what her burgeoning business has delivered. Foremost has been the revelation of the amazing things people are doing for the community and the less fortunate members within it. "I am surrounded by inspiring people, who do things I could only imagine doing and I feel genuinely honoured that my team and I can take care of matters financial so they can get on and do the really important work of helping the community."

At the beginning of 2009, and having achieved her goal of having a business that can function regardless of her being there, she decided to start two new businesses!

The first is as an independent consultant for an organisation specialising in botanically based skin care products. Andrea conducts this business in her 'downtime' and it provides her with an excuse to spend time with lots of women either individually or in groups playing with beauty products.

The second, Women in Balance, is based on the premise that women in their own businesses spend most of their time working and looking after others and need to do things just for themselves whether this be abseiling down the Hilton or doing Tai Chi in the park. In her market research Andrea unearthed a real thirst for low cost networking options for women, particularly those starting out in business, to promote their products and services as well as build relationships with other business women. Andrea's aim is to combine these two concepts to provide relationship building opportunities with an emphasis on fun, education, recreation and adventure.

Andrea's battle with post natal depression has made her keenly aware that life is to be lived as fully as possible and her mission these days is to 'thrive not just survive'.

Her work in the not-for-profit sector as well as Women in Balance is her way of ensuring others are able to do the same.

Heidi Unferdorben

Heroes are found in the most unlikely of places doing the most unlikely of things. What makes them heroes is they don't stop when all the signs are screaming that the game is over.

Heidi Unferdorben works with young teens identified as being at risk of leaving school early and who would benefit from the support a mentor can provide.

But years ago when Heidi started this journey she found many young people were trapped by their lack of options.

As a child Heidi was inspired to "do something" when she saw images of starving African children on her television, without having a clue what it was she could do. But the fire had been lit and when, as an adult, she started working with these young people, she recognised here was an opportunity to "do something".

What she did was become involved in a new, statewide mentoring program to support young people remain connected to their schooling.

"Prisons are full of adults who dropped out of school early and who hate their parents. Also you are at greater risk of poor health if you drop out of school early," informs Heidi with the clarity of an academic explaining a phenomenon.

"So naturally, what we aim to do, is keep young people at school for as long as possible and perhaps more importantly, give them an adult figure they respect and who respects them."

Worthwhile aims, and most reasonable people would agree it's better to help teens than to build more prisons and health care facilities. The program had an army of 400 volunteers mentoring at least that many children from 40 schools around the State.

Then, the funding was significantly cut but Heidi soldiered on and continued to work with her volunteers and the children in need.

"How can you walk away?" asks Heidi rhetorically, "These were children at risk through no fault of theirs. They were hindered by their life circumstances. The volunteer mentors were prepared to stay and I was not going to let them or the young people down."

As an adult she had the capacity to stay and fight and, in some small way, compensate for the little girl who felt helpless when faced with the plight of vulnerable African children.

By continuing to do what she'd started, Heidi, with the support of five local schools, helped to work her way back into the community, corporate and Government conscience and this year funding was provided for a mentoring program to focus on the inner northern suburbs with plans to expand across SA in 2010 and beyond.

But funding is only part of the solution. The key to resolving the dilemma faced by many young people is acceptance, says Heidi. "We, as adults, have to accept these teens just the way they are because it is only through acceptance that we give them back their sense of worth and allow them to believe anything is possible, and at the same time we are trying to teach the teens to accept their parents, whether they are active in their lives or not, and if nothing else, to be grateful for the gift of life they've received and definitely deserve."

The silver lining on the dark cloud of vulnerable teens has been the continuation of the mentoring program once the teenager has completed school.

"To be part of our program you need to be at school, but once you complete school and are 18, if the graduate and the mentor are happy to continue the relationship then that can only be for the benefit of society."

Amanda Horne

Wouldn't we all love to be important enough to have our very own personal assistant running around doing all those necessary but oh so mundane jobs that we really couldn't be bothered doing?

Well, Amanda Horne some time ago recognised not only just how important each and every one of us is, but how much sweeter our lives would be if there was somebody reliable to ensure there were no slip ups in taking care of the everyday tasks in our lives.

It was while working in high level office administration, in such diverse employment sectors as large corporations, SMEs, the public service and even the Office of SA Premier, Mike Rann, that she thought of the idea. She noticed the constant, agitated buzz that seemed to hover over people who had small errands to run that might well be vital to the day-to-day running of their households but seemingly contributed nothing to their workday activity other than a nuisance factor if they didn't get seen to.

"Wouldn't it be wonderful," she thought to herself, "if somebody could go around lifting that burden off these people so they can work uninterrupted?" The answer that came back to her loud and clear was a resounding yes and the even louder message was that the someone was her.

But as anyone who has started a new business knows, there is often a big step between an idea and the execution of that idea and Amanda needed to know she wasn't stepping into a void. Working in her favour was the fact that in spite of all the world's technological advances and gadgets invented to supposedly lessen their work load, people were still incredibly busy and getting even more so as time went on.

So she set up Every Day PA which, as the name suggests, operates as your personal assistant on a daily basis.

Every Day PA came into being in 2007 but Amanda is nothing if not thorough and has in her possession a strategic development plan that stretches all the way to 2018!

"I developed the business based on two premises," explains Amanda, "the first was that people were incredibly busy and would rather spend their time doing things other than the mundane, and the second was putting a value on the efficient administration of the home."

She knew how hard women at home worked and how invisible they were – unpaid and unappreciated – and where most people saw nothing thanks to the cloak of invisibility, Amanda saw opportunity.

It was a simple idea that (strangely enough) resonated with women and men who appreciated their wives. Amanda hopes the legacy of Every Day PA will be to give mums and wives a sense of their own worth not only by undertaking the difficult task of actually costing the value of the services of a stay-at-home wife or mother but by, in fact, employing those wives and mothers to actually do the tasks for her clients.

Her helper mums are called "life assistants" but the many who use them think of them as life savers! Amanda's focus in the New Year will be on the promotion of her Magic Box, a simple idea that will revolutionise household management. Into the box goes everything a personal assistant should handle and once it's in the box, Every Day PA makes sure it gets done, from bills to be paid to dry cleaning to be collected.

For perfectionist Amanda the biggest challenge has been launching Every Day PA despite her need to tweak the system to even greater levels of efficiency. "As we grow the service improves," she concedes, "and by delivering efficiency we enable our customers to operate more efficiently.

It's a win all around!"

Tanya Cole

Tanya Cole would like to be known as the architect of the Nanny State. Not that she's at all over-protective, because the Nanny State she's talking about has nothing to do with overly officious governments and everything to do with building the brand NannySA into one of the State's most recognisable motifs.

We've all heard the mantras – *children are our future* and *who's looking after the children?* – and other bon mots alluding to our collective responsibility for our children. Well Tanya has managed through a touch of curiosity and a big dose of fabulous business acumen to harness our anxiety over our children into a thriving empire.

NannySA and its affiliated companies, Bubble'n'Squeak Child Development Centres, Enhance Recruitment and Enhance Training employs a staggering 400 people across its many locations that spread all the way up to Port Pirie and Port Augusta.

Before Tanya wandered with some trepidation into the nanny business, she cut her teeth in several other ventures including the beautifully named The Big Squeeze (a fresh juice bar enterprise that preceded and was similar in a lot of respects to Boost Juice). "We were three years too early with that concept," recalls Tanya, "and when it folded I returned to full time employment to support myself and my two children."

But you can't keep a good businesswoman off the track for any length of time and before long Tanya had started a corporate cleaning business that introduced her to the world of night shift. A few years later Tanya spotted an advertisement for a nanny franchise business and for nine months represented the international chain in SA before they parted ways.

However, it certainly wasn't a wasted experience as Tanya used what she'd learned to launch NannySA.

Initially it was purely a service offering nannies but as Tanya observed: "As you learn more about the business you're in you discover more opportunities."

The opportunities Tanya discovered included the need to train and qualify nannies and even unearthed the world of emergency carers who were charged with caring for children under guardianship. This service required NannySA to provide what's called pseudo parenting to children in need.

The carers would provide 24 hour supervision in shifts to fully answer the question – who's looking after the children? A further adjunct to this side of the business was responding to the government's call to mentor youths in residential care.

While it wasn't a world Tanya envisaged when she took her first nanny booking, it was a world to which she responded magnificently and grew her businesses while fulfilling a very real need. Taking courses with Robert Kiyosaki gave her the confidence to sell her house to invest big time in NannySA thinking "I can do this". And she certainly could.

The longer Tanya stayed in the child care business the more she discovered the extent to which she was needed.

When the ABC Child Care Centres collapsed, Tanya, in partnership, bought six of them and has steadily been rebuilding them as going concerns after they had suffered a severe slump because of lack of public confidence following the collapse.

She rebranded the facilities as Bubble'n'Squeak Child Development Centres and through the application of proven systems and well respected business practices, has restored them to health.

Consciously or not, it's all part of fulfilling Tanya's motto of leaving the world in better shape than you find it. She describes her incredible journey as a "very nice adventure" and is grateful for the opportunity to indulge her passion – working with and helping develop the potential of people.

Kylie Bishop

Kylie Bishop, by her own admission, is greedy for life. She wanted it all, career and children, says the high-heeled corporate high flyer who gets around in pink Ugg boots when she's at home, enjoying "the best life ever".

The journey that makes her life today taste so sweet was fraught with challenges, disappointment and danger but whenever she confronted one of these impostors she turned them into triumphs because that's simply her way.

While Kylie is a qualified accountant, she credits her five children with schooling her for success. "To succeed in business you need to be able to negotiate, to communicate and then to deliver," says Kylie, "and nothing teaches you those skills more effectively than dealing with children!"

Kylie's children fall into two sets, three while she was a very young person with her first husband and two slightly later in life with her second husband.

While for many people dealing with fractured families can be a source of enormous stress and even tragedy, Kylie has made a "close friend" of her first husband who remains an integral part of her life and is like an uncle to Kylie's two children with her second husband!

Her second husband, for his part, is of equally generous spirit and embraces every part of Kylie's past to make for a large and happy, albeit hectic, family unit.

The somewhat unusual dynamics of her family life are crucial to her success in the corporate world because Kylie has used it as a model when it comes to managing her relationships with her clients, business partners and staff.

"We are accountable," says Kylie, "as parents we are responsible for the quality of family life we provide for our children and as corporate providers of a vital service we ensure we are not only diligent in the execution of our duties but also open in our communication, so that the relationships only get stronger.

"I certainly try very hard to run my business with the passion and enthusiasm I lavish on my family," confesses Kylie. Both her family and her business have seven people although Kylie is positive that the only room for growth is in the business!

The business she nurtures is LBW Environment, a boutique environmental consultancy specialising in contaminated land and water issues, where her husband is the managing director and principal scientist, she is the general manager and her ex-husband's firm is the external accountant!

Developers who might have acquired contaminated land turn to LBW for help in preparing the land for residential use, and larger companies engage LBW as a trusted adviser and to monitor for compliance with environmental legislation and guidelines.

LBW's competition in the area of environmental management are companies that employ hundreds of people in SA, but Kylie is finding more clients are turning to LBW because they like the service and can talk directly to owners of the company.

"I grew up in larger engineering and environmental consulting firms and got to a point where I wanted to offer a more personalised service genuinely focused on understanding and meeting the needs of the client, while balancing the demands of our family" she explains.

Just as she was about to launch LBW with her husband, Kylie was diagnosed with thyroid cancer. "I haven't got the time to have cancer," she thought, so with a combination of good luck and diligence she beat it.

To stay healthy and to help keep her life in perspective Kylie has taught herself to slow down and enjoy the moment.

She sits down to eat breakfast every morning and cooks for her tribe almost every night – replete in pink Ugg boots!

Emma Wallace

Sometimes an idea is so simple you're kicking yourself all the way to China because you didn't think it up.

For years Emma Wallace harboured a passion for real estate but despite being courted and doing a thorough investigation of the options available, she never found a company that was a right fit for her. To pinpoint the reasons for the mismatch was about as hard as getting a straight answer from a conventional real estate agent.

Then one day, not so long ago, while holidaying in Queensland she saw a company with a catchy logo and started to look a bit deeper. What she found was a system with which she could work and the magic ingredient that made this particular methodology so darned attractive was two words – fixed commission.

"It meant that as an agent you no longer had to play games with the vendor," she says. For Emma it lifted the sense of shady from being an agent and allowed her to do what she always felt was the agent's real task – selling the house, rather than using the opportunity of selling as an excuse to fish for more vendors.

"I thought, at last, here's a system that frees up agents from the tyranny of commissions," recalls Emma but before she invested in bringing Go Gecko to Adelaide, she signed up to work as an agent in Queensland. "I wanted to make sure it was all above board and there were no downsides that might make me regret being associated with the company."

For two years Emma worked as a Go Gecko agent in Queensland and all she witnessed in that time was the incredible success of the brand and how, by working for a fixed commission with an ethical company it "obliterated the need to lie".

But while it certainly made her feel good being involved with a feel good organisation, it was the inroads Go Gecko was making in the market that excited the entrepreneur within.

"When we started, the initiators of Go Gecko felt a 4% market share would be a decent slice, but within a very short time they had revised that estimate up to a staggering 30%!"

But, as happens so often, just when it looks as if life couldn't get any better, it gets decidedly worse. Emma's hubby did his back in playing rugby and was immobilised. With two young children and still breast feeding her youngest, Emma not only sat for and acquired her real estate license but also thoroughly tested the sales system of Go Gecko.

She loved it but needed to get back to her support base in Adelaide and the family moved here and brought Go Gecko with them.

In Adelaide, Emma has taken on three girlfriends as partners to run the office at Glenelg and the team plans to open another seven offices throughout the Adelaide metropolitan area in the next few years. With hubby undergoing a back fusion and slowly returning to full health, Emma has a fulltime house husband and is relishing the freedom to grow a brand she is proud to own.

"I inherited my strong sense of social justice from my Irish father who rose from an impoverished beginning to put himself through Harvard before migrating to Rhodesia (now Zimbabwe) where I was born and from there to Australia."

Emma regards her integrity as her strongest quality and would like to be remembered as someone who helped contribute to ease the suffering of people less fortunate.

While that might be a little way in the future she would at least like to start by removing the pain of uncertainty from real estate dealing.

Priscilla Bokhara

Nudity is a subject close to Priscilla Bokhara's heart. Emotional nudity, that is, where you stand stripped of all pretension, without any mask to hide behind.

What you see when you look at her emotionally naked is what you get.

Her past is a matter of record. As a child of 8 she was molested by a family friend, her parents divorced at the age of 10, she started going to Alcoholics Anonymous at the age of 11 so she could better understand her mother. She was hit by a car at 12 and spent 8 months in a plaster cast.

Finally, when she was 25, the man who spoke of marriage to her the day before, jumped out of a hotel window to his death while she was the only other person in the room. Then the voice from within – a peaceful warrior spirit – spoke to her, loudly and clearly, and urged her to go on living.

In the 15 years since she has packed more into her life than most people manage in 100 years. She has penned her own Seven Truths of Abundance that she calls on to empower herself and those in her considerable circle of influence.

What Priscilla has learned is she's here to serve and being a servant is the highest point a person can reach. "From my time at AA and from the lessons since I have learned it's not what's right or wrong but what's real for people.

If I believe, as I do, I became my best when I was simply *being* me, why would I try to get others to change? It is only through *being* who they truly are that they will shine."

Priscilla is a highly in-demand personal coach, with her inspirational insights and spiritually neutral delivery that is both supportive and non-judgmental and a conversation with her is littered with quotable quotes that deserve to be recorded and pinned in places where they can act as daily reminders.

"Every decision I make in a state of joy is *always* the best decision," is one that flows from her as naturally as a melting mountain stream.

The message she communicates is the special person you seek is the one you *already* are, the importance of celebrating life and giving yourself permission to shine.

The impermanence of life was again brought home to Priscilla when her elder sister, Kathleen, came down with breast cancer and Priscilla was desperate to do something to help.

That something turned out to be the phenomenon known as Bouncing for Breast Cancer and Priscilla took her trampoline with her to such notable sites as the Taj Mahal, the Eiffel Tower, the Leaning Tower of Pisa and the 12 Apostles and was photographed and filmed bouncing in front of these landmarks to help raise awareness of the condition and some much-needed money for her sister's treatment.

After a single mastectomy, Kathleen is fully recovered and Priscilla is looking for someone to take over the running of the hugely popular project that has the ability to help the thousands of single mothers who find themselves in similar circumstances every year.

It's not that she wants to walk away from something positive she created, but her energies are demanded elsewhere where she is focused on helping create happier, healthier and wealthier people every day through her personal development programs and sharing the gift of a leading Swiss anti-aging skin care product that is booming in Australia.

As this once restless soul relaxes in her Stirling haven, she muses: "Someone once told me, when you get there, you'll *know*. Now I feel as if I've arrived."

Lucy MacGill

With a name tailor-made for a country and western song, Lucy MacGill added to the legend when she designed a range of clothes called Angel Wings inspired by a close friend who had died unexpectedly.

But, as with any good story, it starts with the heartbreak of a failed relationship and a young girl being left with twin boys less than a year old and only her talent to call on.

It was a time for Lucy to do what she knew she did best even if that meant straining the relationship with her babies so, for the next three years she and they did it tough as mum worked every waking hour to create a future where she could be the mum she always wanted to be.

Today the boys are 10 and one night recently they were talking about the tough times and they confirmed what mum knew, it had been hard on them and they had missed her. But now she was here and everything was going to be all right.

As the song ends Lucy remembers a refrain that was played out a few years earlier when she boarded an airplane the day a story appeared in a local newspaper about this very battle.

"An air hostess whispered to me she had seen the story in the paper that day and no one else on the plane knew but she was pregnant and she said my story had so inspired her she had decided to keep the baby she had been planning to give up for adoption.

"Yeah," added Lucy in a tired drawl as she remembered the day, "everyone has roads they have to walk."

She is happy that her life today is all about her children, her beautiful boys and the wonderful man who came into her life to create the happy ending, but Lucy MacGill is far from finished with all that she needs to do in life.

Her brand Angel Wings, inspired by her dear friend Mark Kerghery, who the fashion conscious might know as Mark of Marcs fame who helped popularise the Diesel brand of jeans (with Lucy's help) is now in 60 high-end fashion outlets around the country and its output has increased by a staggering 400% in little more than a year, while as Lucy MacGill Agencies, Lucy represents a number of high-end fashion labels in SA.

While there's little doubt Melbourne and Sydney are widely considered the fashion capitals of Australia and Lucy worked in both cities establishing herself, once she became a single mum she headed home to be near her support base. "I was tired of searching and I needed to set us up," said Lucy referring to her family of three.

While here she established Platinum just at the time Adelaide had turned "hot and stylish" as people discovered brands and young women were not afraid to flaunt their beauty.

"The year was 2001 and the business just took off," remembers Lucy and once it had hit its peak she sold Platinum so she could devote more time to her sons.

But a girl still needs to work and Lucy tapped into her considerable contacts to establish her agency and once that was humming, she stretched her wings to create what will become an iconic brand.

And if that is not enough, Lucy has yet another business called Wardrobe Therapy where she consults as a fashion stylist. "I only throw out some clothes and we replace them with selected items we can mix and match to keep you stylish.

"Every woman deserves to look stylish," sighs this earth-bound angel.

Kylie Jacobs

Kylie Jacobs pinches herself every morning because she can't quite believe what is happening. Fortunately it's all good, and she's not trying to wake up from any nightmare.

No, Kylie developed a brand that is about to kick serious butt. A lot of people know Female Friendly, the accreditation process that gives the pink tick to businesses that prove they treat women with honesty, decency and integrity.

It's a brand devised by Kylie and launched by her and her sisters, Caroline Davis and Elizabeth Grace in 2007 and now has 400 businesses nationally signed up and more than 4000 Friends of Female Friendly.

The brand is so popular that at a recent girls' night out in Adelaide, 2500 women turned up ready to party and keen to spread the word.

Well, all that is about to change and Kylie hopes for the better because her brand is about to get even more powerful thanks to an alliance she has formed with prominent Port Lincoln businesswoman, Christine Santic, also known as the owner of a horse that won a few races. You might remember it, called Makybe Diva which trotted home ahead of the rest in three consecutive Melbourne Cups.

Well Christine has decided to throw her considerable influence behind Female Friendly, loves the brand and is determined to make it grow more powerful to better serve the needs of women everywhere.

Kylie and Christine have an amazing team busily working behind the scenes preparing to launch the Female Friendly Wellness range specifically designed to energise and emotionally uplift women naturally. It is one of several initiatives planned for the brand.

So now you can understand why Kylie pinches herself on a daily basis.

It seems so long ago that Kylie, whose motto is "anything but housework" was looking to start something so she could get out of housework. But, as the book keeper and manager of her husband's tyre and mechanic shop she ensured it was always pristine. Customers took note and started commenting and Kylie got an idea. "If women like the way this shop is presented and it keeps them coming back, maybe other businesses that are tying to appeal to women need to know what I know!"

Kylie was doing little more than keeping the place clean, having up-to-date family friendly magazines in the waiting room, making sure the pile of children's toys were always tidied after a family left – the sort of things you might do when you're expecting visitors so they don't think you're an absolute slob.

So determined was Kylie to achieve her business dream (and get out of housework) she and her sisters worked hard in developing a system that accredited businesses prepared to do the small things to make women feel comfortable and slowly, slowly it grew.

Oh sure, Kylie had her battles, and life with four children under seven juggling her motherhood responsibilities with her burgeoning business was never going to be easy. Fortunately she had a supportive husband who could see the big picture and did his darndest to enable his entrepreneurial wife to make her mark which, by this time, was a big pink tick.

As Female Friendly becomes even more friendly, Kylie wants to encourage and support women to realise what they are capable of. "We tend to underestimate ourselves," observes Kylie, "and we need to understand the greatest challenge is to get started. So long as you have a plan, you can do anything."

Kylie's plans include finally building a family home so the children don't have to sleep in the lounge and rewarding the family for tolerating her by taking them all to Disneyland for her 40th birthday. She's got 18 months but she's already almost there.

"The notion that by succeeding academically or later, by succeeding in any management, you therefore destroy your femininity' is the most pervasive threat against women."

MARY WARNOCK (B. 1924)
BRITISH PHILOSOPHER AND AUTHOR
SPEECH, INSTITUTE OF DIRECTORS, LONDON (25TH NOVEMBER 1985)

111 Amanda Horne
Everyday PA
www.
everydaypa.
com.au

107 Andrea Petersen
Not for Profit
Accounting
www.nfpas.
com.au

17 Christine Jenner
Foundation
Daw Park
www.
foundationpark.
org.au

109 Heidi Unferdorben
Community
Mentoring
www.youth
mentoring.org.au

27 Karen Norris
Botanic Photos
www.
botanicphotos.
com

53 Angelique Boileau
Boileau Business
Solutions
www.boileau.
com.au

45 Belinda & Cheryl
My Wedding
Magazine
www.my
weddingmag.
com.au

47 Christine Robinson
Barossa Valley
Global Enterprise
www.
christinerobinson.
com.au

55 Deborah Miller
Acuere
www.acuere.
com.au

83 Irena Zhang
Novaline Furniture
www.
novalinefurniture.
com.au

33 Joanna Politis
A Touch of
Beauty
www.atouch
ofbeauty-sa.
com.au

101 Kathy Fullston
Cloverland
Organics
www.cloverland
organics.
com.au

91 Ann Grenci
TAFE
www.
tafesa.
com.au

67 Blis Bohunnis
Acqua Blis
www.
acquablis.
com.au

99 Colette Smith
Telstra
Corporation Ltd
www.
telstra.
com.au

103 Donny Walford
DW Bottom
Line
www.
dwbottomline.
com.au

71 Jan Wood
Heathcare
Specialty Prods
www.
healthspec.
com.au

75 Judy Hamilton
Ultimate
Dynamics Institute
www.
judyhamilton.
com.au

21 Kelly Keates
Zonge Engineering
& Research Org
www.
zonge.
com.au

61 Bec Paris-Hewitt
Zootz Kitchen
Bar
www.
zootz.
com.au

25 Charyn Youngson
Houses to
Impress
www.
housestoimpress.
com.au

117 Corina Kowald
I am Tall Poppy
www.unique
luxurygifts.
com.au

73 Emma Wallace
Go Gecko
www.
gogecko.
com.au

89 Jan Wood

63 Jing Lee
Asia Pacific
Council
www.
apbcw.
com

13 Karen Martin
Aus Cntr for Ntrl
Hlth & Wllness
www.
acnhw.
com.au

Kerrie Akkerman
Akkermans
Consulting
www.akkermans
consulting.
com.au

115 Kylie Bishop
LBW
Environment P/L
www.lbw
environment.
com.au

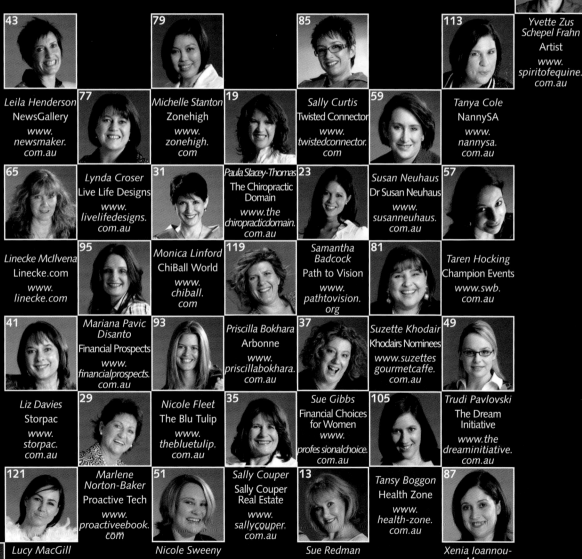

15
Yvette Zus
Schepel Frahn
Artist
www.
spiritofequine.
com.au

43
Leila Henderson
NewsGallery
www.
newsmaker.
com.au

77
Michelle Stanton
Zonehigh
www.
zonehigh.
com

79

19

85
Sally Curtis
Twisted Connector
www.
twistedconnector.
com

59
Tanya Cole
NannySA
www.
nannysa.
com.au

113

65
Lynda Croser
Live Life Designs
www.
livelifedesigns.
com.au

31
Paula Stacey-Thomas
The Chiropractic
Domain
www.the
chiropracticdomain.
com.au

23
Susan Neuhaus
Dr Susan Neuhaus
www.
susanneuhaus.
com.au

57

95
Linecke McIlvena
Linecke.com
www.
linecke.com

Monica Linford
ChiBall World
www.
chiball.
com

119
Samantha
Badcock
Path to Vision
www.
pathtovision.
org

81
Taren Hocking
Champion Events
www.swb.
com.au

41
Mariana Pavic
Disanto
Financial Prospects
www.
financialprospects.
com.au

93
Priscilla Bokhara
Arbonne
www.
priscillabokhara.
com.au

37
Suzette Khodair
Khodairs Nominees
www.suzettes
gourmetcaffe.
com.au

49

Liz Davies
Storpac
www.
storpac.
com.au

29
Nicole Fleet
The Blu Tulip
www.
thebluetulip.
com.au

35
Sue Gibbs
Financial Choices
for Women
www.
profes sionalchoice.
com.au

105
Trudi Pavlovski
The Dream
Initiative
www.the
dreaminitiative.
com.au

121
Marlene
Norton-Baker
Proactive Tech
www.
proactiveebook.
com

51
Sally Couper
Sally Couper
Real Estate
www.
sallycouper.
com.au

13
Tansy Boggon
Health Zone
www.
health-zone.
com.au

87

123

Lucy MacGill
Lucy Macgill
Agencies
www.
lucymacgill.
com.au

Nicole Sweeny
Revolution
Consulting
www.
revcon.
com.au

Sue Redman
Lunches with
Sue Redman
www.
sueredman.
com.au

Xenia Ioannou-
Mena
AdProp.com.au
www.
adprop.
com.au

Thank you

From the time I hit the send button on the email announcing 'Nominations Open' for Lounge to Boardroom, it was exactly 2 months to the day that we ended with our pre-launch soirée and page selection lottery.

This was a MAMMOTH task of epic proportions which no publisher in their right mind would attempt to pull off. To herd and shepherd 55 strong-willed women to photo-shoots, have their interviews and to ensure they met their sign off deadlines and to get them all in the same room at the same time for their page selection was an enormous ask.

But we did it! Though not without help.

And so, I would like to thank the following, who helped keep this project on time, on the rails, within budget and kept me sane!

Emma - she was Sergeant Majorish in her approach and she kept the wheels in motion - but she got it done.

Ben - who slaved behind the camera to be UBER creative with every shot and captured the essence of all the ladies.

Andrew - who slept at his keyboard for 3 weeks solid and despite being sleep deprived, still wrote magnificent stories about the ladies - by golly he did it!

Kara - who made all the ladies feel comfortable and look beautiful.

Our judges - Alex, Nick & Emma, who had the hardest task of choosing from so many women - rather you than me!

Paul Atkins - from Atkins Technicolour who so generously provided the gorgeous prints for the ladies to keep as a memento.

Bec Paris-Hewitt - who graciously hosted the pre-launch soirée at Zootz.

Loana Liew - whose eagle eye spotted even the tiniest typo.

The Lounge to Boardroom ladies - who dared to follow me in my vision and dip their toes in unchartered waters.

Our readers - for believing in this book and finding inspiration within these pages.

And last but certainly not least, my darling husband Dale, who kept us in tea, was a gofer, kept the IT systems running smoothly and was there every step of the way.

Thank you - Ashley

ashley
KNOOTE-PARKE